The Trade Show Chronicles

2nd edition

JULIEN RIO

ISBN-10:1542721032
ISBN-13:978-1542721035

INTRODUCTION

The Trade Show Chronicles is a fiction based on real events.

Andrew is a fictional character; yet, many aspects of his story come from my own experience.
I moved to Hong Kong a decade ago and worked in marketing across multiple industries: logistics, electronics, hospitality, apps, toys, medical, cleaning, events, manufacturing, etc. Almost immediately, I entered the world of trade shows, organizing booths for my company at different exhibitions around the world and often being in the booth, dealing with visitors then managing the follow-ups for the whole team.

The very first time I was put in charge of our booth, I had little to no knowledge of what trade shows were all about. I was dynamic and eager to take on additional responsibilities so I did not reject the challenge - I spent weeks reading books and online articles to figure out what I was really supposed to do. Each day had a new surprise, a new difficulty for me to overcome. From reading lengthy and messy exhibitor manuals to dealing with uncooperative suppliers, I faced all the problems you could imagine organizing your first event.

When the opening day finally arrived, I was really excited. Talking with visitors was a great opportunity for me to really face our customers and better understand their needs. I was also really keen on receiving praises for my good work setting up the whole booth, but I quickly realized that no-one actually knew the amount of work that I had to put into it. It was as if people believed the stall just grew on its own.

After three exhausting days in the booth I was full of energy - my feet were in pain, my brain was crying for more caffeine and my eyes were half closed, but I was satisfied and excited. I had made it. I was given an impossible mission with almost no support, but I made it. It was a great success and my boss congratulated me for the good job.

I thought it was over, that I would go back to my normal marketing life. But the following Monday, my boss brought me a large pile of "fair reports" - A4 paper sheets covered with hand-written notes from every staff in the booth. I was now in charge of reading, filtering and organizing the leads.
It took me a week to decipher as much as I possibly could and transfer it to digital. I tried my very best to arrange everything in the same format, then I passed the result of my hard work back to my boss.

All I could hear for the following days were complaints. "Why is this lead incomplete? Where is the phone number? What is the next step with this one? There is no name on that report!"
I was being blamed for not providing the full information, even though it wasn't me taking the notes in the first place.

Ultimately, most of the leads were followed-up about 2 weeks after the show. Many of them ended up in the trash because the person in charge of following-up considered there wasn't enough information to write an efficient email.

I quietly observed the fruit of my hard work being wasted. Ultimately, not a single contract was signed as a result of the show. We had invested thousands of dollars for zero results, but everyone seemed very content with the outcome.

Behind my boss' back I could hear my colleagues' sarcastic remarks: "Great, we are going to a trade show next month! What a great way to spend some money!"

I am analytical. I can't just give up without understanding the reasons of a failure. So I started writing a checklist of everything that went wrong and how it could have been prevented. It was quickly obvious that the show could have been a terrific opportunity if a few details had been handled differently.

Show after show I started improving my techniques, learning from my mistakes and taking notes to always get better.

A few years later, after an incredible adventure as Head of Marketing for a fast growing startup, I decided to make use of my knowledge to improve the trade show industry. I first created myfairtool, a complete online solution for companies participating in trade shows. My goal was to provide people like me, organizing booth on behalf of their company, with efficient tools that would boost their efficiency, reduce their workload and increase their outcome. I built myfairtool so it could be everything I wish I had back when I organized my first show: a clear guideline, an efficient promotion tool, a system to better capture and follow-up on leads and convert prospects into customers.

Soon after, I started writing the Trade Show Chronicles. I did not want another boring book written like a checklist of dos & don'ts that people go through and forget. I wanted to write a story. I wanted to engage people on a different level, put them in the shoes of Andrew, and walk them through the whole journey of organizing a trade show booth.

The Trade Show Chronicles were originally shared chapter by chapter on myfairtool's blog (The Exhibitor) then reworked and turned into a real book that would help anyone become a trade show expert.

Whether you are facing your first exhibition or are an expert with 30 years experience, there is always something to learn. Share this book with everyone in your trade show planning team and start building a powerful strategy to optimize your return on investment.

I sincerely hope you will enjoy reading it and that it will help you better manage your future events.

Julien Rio.

The Trade Show Chronicles

CONTENTS

ACKNOWLEDGMENTS

I would like to express my gratitude to the people who saw me through this book. I would like to thank Marius for his help revising and improving The Trade Show Chronicles, Royce and Wilson for their talent designing the right cover, and my wife, Angela, for her continuous and unwavering support.

Chapter 1.
MY FIRST EXHIBITION

I have recently joined Global Tech Ltd. as a Sales Executive. Every day I follow a contact list provided by my marketing team and make calls to all these people, trying to arrange meetings. Every afternoon, I go out and meet with existing clients and potential new customers. I use a CRM that we've developed in-house to record information about my customers.

Last month, my boss informed the whole team that we were about to join the HKTDC Hong Kong Electronics Fair later this year. He seemed very excited about it and said that was an incredible opportunity for us to present our new products to the world and reach new customers. I did not pay too much attention to it: just another marketing event. Not really my concern.

A few days later, he called me in for a one-to-one meeting.

– "Andrew, what do you know about the Electronics Fair?" I did not expect we would discuss this topic.

– "I don't know much about it… It is a marketing event made to present new products, right?"

– "Yes and no. Trade shows are not 'marketing' events. They are marketing & sales events. They are a great opportunity for you to meet with new suppliers, customers, investors or even competitors. They are especially good for you to generate leads and attack new unexplored markets."

– "Well… I didn't know that", I say a bit puzzled, wondering how that concerns me. "I have never joined such an event before."

– "Andrew, I want you to be the lead and organize our participation to the HKTDC Hong Kong Electronics Fair."

I felt my heart stopped beating for a second.

I only have one year of experience and all I have ever worked on so far was sales focused. That's what I know and what I do. I have no knowledge whatsoever about "exhibitions" or "trade shows". Why ME? Why should I organize a marketing event?

– "Well… Wouldn't the marketing team be more…"

He does not let me finish:

– "As I told you, this isn't a marketing event. Our marketing team has organized it for the past 4 years with a clear marketing objective: brand awareness. This year, I want to articulate it around a real business objective: collecting valuable leads that could then be followed-up by yourself and transformed into customers. Don't worry, the marketing folks will guide you and provide all possible help when it comes to design and promotion."

Design? Promotion? I did not even think about that! Why does he seem so excited about me organizing it? I've never done such a thing before. This will for sure end badly!

– "So, Andrew, what's your answer? Can I count on you?" he asks with a large smile.

– "Absolutely!" I hear myself say, without a clue of what that implies.

That night I couldn't sleep. I thought my job was difficult enough without having to put more responsibilities on my shoulders.

I spent most of the next day researching what a trade show really is and where I should start. The opening was only 6 months away and I had absolutely no idea about what was expected of me.

I read article after article, blog after blog, looking for the perfect recipe I could simply apply to succeed. I started to have a better idea about the concept: a giant hall, hundreds of companies having decorated stalls and presenting their products, tons of visitors from the same industry coming to see the new trends and buy some products, some media looking for the innovation that could make a buzz, competitors searching for ideas to copy or improve, investors analyzing opportunities and a lot a flyers, business cards, luggage and samples running around. And me.

Without any knowledge of this overwhelming industry that is *event*, I am in charge of organizing a portion of it. Quite despaired, I look at my phone: 23:02. I have spent an entire day researching for this project, neglecting my usual tasks, and it doesn't feel like I have made any progress.

Suddenly, I remember that one of my old schoolmates from high school mentioned something interesting last time, during our annual dinner. It seems he has become specialist in exhibitions: event planner or something of that sort. I start dialing his number but I cut the line before the first ring: kind of late to bother people you don't really talk to that often. I decide to call back on the next day and head to bed.

A minute later, my phone rings:

– "Hey Andrew, you called me? What's up?"

Chapter 2.
FINDING THE RIGHT GOAL

– "Hi Charles! Sorry to bother you that late. It's just…
Look, I have been dragged into a new project recently. I'm
now in charge of the organization of my company's booth
for the HKTDC Hong Kong Electronics Fair and I seem
to remember you are specialized in this."
– "Congratulations! You must be very excited! That's quite
a project you've got yourself in!"
– "Well… I wouldn't say I'm 'excited', more like worried
really. I have never done this before and I just don't know
where to start. I thought… you know, maybe you could
give me a hand on that."
– "Look buddy, I'd love to help you out, but event
organization can't be taught in the blink of an eye. It took
me years to get where I am and I happen to have a flight
early tomorrow morning. I'm flying to Singapore for
another event."
– "Ok… I understand, no worries."
– "Look, I don't have time to give you a full overview of

5

how to plan an event properly, but I can definitely help you out a little. Organizing a trade show isn't complicated: it is very much like a puzzle. First you have to get all the pieces right then you assemble them together to get the full picture."

– "Right…" I say, half convinced, "so what are these pieces you're talking about?"

– "Your event is very much divided into three periods: before, during, after. Your first challenge will be to define your ultimate goal: why are your organizing that event? Once you get this right, you will need to find out what you should do at each stage (before, during, after) in order to reach that target."

What is he talking about? I am looking for practical advice, not riddles.

– "Well, that's pretty obvious, right? My objective is to organize the event because my boss asked me so." I say impatiently.

– "Is that right? Would your boss ask you to organize an event for the sake of organizing an event? Why did he ask you, a sales person, to do it instead of your marketing team? Look Andrew, it was real nice talking to you, but I need to sleep now. Give me a call when you find your answers!"

Back to square one. What just happened? Charles might be an expert in his field but I still don't have much of a clue about what I should be doing now. Before, during, after?

Before I must organize the show, during I must be there and after I can just sit back and relax. Isn't it?

And what did Charles mean about "the goal"?

If the event in itself isn't the goal, then why organize it? It seems my boss mentioned something about it... "brand awareness". That could be the goal! I should call back Charles and tell him about it!

Hold on... He also asked why I was suddenly in charge of the project. Could that have something to do with a change of purpose...?

As a sales person, my goal is to sell. Right, sounds easy enough! The goal of this trade show is for me to sign a lot of contracts. So I should prepare the contracts and products before the event, sell on the spot and... well... there isn't really anything to do after the fair. Prepare for the next one maybe?

On the next day my boss calls me and Karen, the girl in charge of marketing, for a meeting.

– "Ok Andrew, how are things going with the Electronics Fair? Have you chosen the booth yet?"

Chosen the booth? I was supposed to choose the booth myself?

A complete week has passed since he put me in charge and I must say not much has been done since. I have defined my goal – selling – and started to draft contracts but that's about it. What did he expect me to do?

– "Huh. No, I haven't chosen the booth yet, but I was about to do it." I lie, not really convincing. "I got the contracts ready though", I say enthusiastically.
– "Contracts? What contracts?"
– "For the fair! To sell right on the spot!"
– "Andrew, I know you haven't had a chance to attend any exhibition before, but you won't have much opportunity to sign contracts there. People go there to see new products, make connections, evaluate the market and get some prices… They are not yet at this stage of the sales funnel. You'd be very lucky to sign a single contract!"

Wow. It seems I got it all wrong! Charles just put me on the wrong path here… I should have had my booth ready by now, instead I've spent a week preparing a contract that no-one will use. How am I supposed to guess the next steps if no-one tells me?

– "So what's your next step then? Did you discuss the checklist with Karen yet?"

Karen looks at me, surprised to hear her name mentioned. I can feel her glaring at me and get less and less comfortable.

– "Well… no, I haven't. I've been quite busy to be honest."
– "Andrew, I put you in charge of this project. Do you have any idea how much the event is going to cost us? We cannot afford to fail. Make it happen!"

He is trying to remain calm, that bit is obvious. I can feel the pressure increasing on my shoulders – I did not even consider the budget! I need to look into this as soon as possible.

After the meeting ends, I talk with Karen to put her in the loop. She sounds very reassuring: she will provide me with a full checklist. She has organized plenty of events in the past few years and seems happy to help me out. She is a little surprised the project wasn't given to her but she seems relieved: preparing for such a large scale event is very time consuming. I decide to ask her what is the ultimate goal of the event.

She looks back at me with a look of absolute disbelief, shakes her head and replies "Brand awareness, obviously" as she turns back and walks away.

Chapter 3.
MY EXHIBITION CHECKLIST

It has been almost two weeks since I have been assigned this project and I still haven't done much. There are five and half months left before the trade show and still a million things to organize. I have my next meeting with the boss and Karen tomorrow and I still haven't picked a location for the booth. I still don't even know what is my true goal.

I decide that it is really time for me to call Charles again.

– "Hey Andrew! How are things on your side?"
– "Hello Charles. Look, I really need your help here. I have an important meeting tomorrow and I don't even know what to do with this event yet!"
– "Have you defined your goal yet?"
– "Yes. My goal is brand awareness."
– "Is this really YOUR goal? Or is it something your marketing team told you?"

How can he possibly know that comes from Karen? I'm getting very frustrated but I decide to play along to see what he has in mind.

– "Well… As a salesperson I'm here to sell… So I would guess my goal should be to sell at the stall, but my boss told me it is very hard to sell at an exhibition… Please, give me some advice here!"
– "Your boss is right: selling at a trade show is very hard. Visitors come to learn things and meet new people. Only a few are ready to buy. But I believe you have the answer already. As you said, you need to sell."

That's it! I understand now, all makes sense! I was wondering why I couldn't find the last piece, what to do AFTER the event. It is now clear to me:

– "My goal is to find prospects so that I could sell to AFTER the exhibition. I need to generate leads!"
– "Congratulations, you found your goal! To be more specific, you need to generate quality leads that will help you in acquiring new customers, but we could focus on this later. What matters now is that you get the basics right. Do you have a checklist of things to prepare for the event?"
– "The marketing team is preparing it for me."
– "That is great. But keep in mind: their goal and yours differ. When you follow the list, ask yourself at each step how it should be done in order for you to achieve your

goal."

– "Thank you very much Charles! Could I call you back later today to discuss this list?"

– "I won't be available for the rest of the day. Start going through your checklist and identify key elements that will help you reach your target. Once that is done, separate them into the three sections I mentioned earlier: before, during, after. Call me back next week, we'll discuss then!"

– "But I would like to…"

Charles already hung up. It seems I'm on my own for tomorrow's meeting, and I'm not really comfortable about it. Good news is, Karen will soon provide me with a short list of what I need to do. That should certainly help me get it right.

Later in the day, Karen pays me a visit with some documents. She's got a very complicated excel file containing a long list of items.

– "Here you go! Simply follow that list step by step and everything will be fine!"

I start going through the trade show organization checklist.

– "That many? I haven't even started working on any of these points! And what is that? Electricity? Lighting? What am I, a craftsman now?"

– "Don't be silly. You must define your needs for an electrician to install items on your booth for you."

– "But… I have no idea about that!"

– "You will have to learn! Go through my list, make sure you don't forget anything and you'll be just fine. Come see me if you need help."

She leaves before I have time to reply. Logistics? Carpets? Reports? Internet? Really? How am I supposed to do all that?

Ok, one step at a time! First, I have to find the right booth location, I have delayed this for too long! Among the pile of documents she left on my desk I find an interesting article that explains how to pick the right place. I need to select a booth in the correct section, preferably on a large alley, in a corner so we could enjoy openings on two sides, and close to a perks section… got it! All I have to do now is call the organizer and make sure this spot is still available!

Chapter 4.
PREPARING THE BASICS

It has now been a month since I was assigned this project. I have already decided which booth to book and I have started to go through the checklist. My boss is getting impatient and during today's meeting I will need to walk him through my progress.

Task after task I start to enjoy this new challenge. Unfortunately, my daily routine has suffered quite a bit and I don't have enough time each day to handle everything. I will have to finish planning the exhibition soon if I want to have a chance of hitting my monthly targets.

I am lost in my thoughts when Karen calls me to join them in the meeting room.

– "So, Andrew, where are we?"
– "The booth's location has been defined and Karen and I started to discuss booth design and…"

– "Walk me through it, don't go in every direction. Have you finalized the announcement?"

– "The announcement? What do you mean by that?"

– "The announcement! We are paying a lot of money to attend this event, you don't plan on announcing it?! The event is only a few months away, you need to announce it now!" he clearly lost his patience this time. I try to keep mine, breathe deeply and reply.

– "Al…right… I will prepare this with Karen right away."

– "Think about your organization as a flow. You have plenty of time to discuss carpet color and intensity of light. You must work on what is most urgent first! Divide your work into sections!"

Suddenly, it strikes me: Charles had mentioned it several times. Before, during, after. I am already planning the "during" part even though I haven't prepared the "before" one!

I present the rest of my progress to our boss and run out to call Charles immediately after.

– "Charles, I need your help!"

– "Hello Andrew, how are you doing?"

– "I think I now understand what you meant. I first need to focus on what happens BEFORE the fair. Once finalized, I will arrange what goes on during the trade show and… what happens afterwards?"

– "Well done! Ignore the "after" for the time being. Have you started to work on 'before' yet? It should be finished by now."

– "That is exactly what my boss told me today! What do you mean by that? What am I supposed to do?"

– "Traffic drives traffic. Try to get as many people as you can in your stall to increase your chances of leads collection and brand awareness."

– "I thought brand awareness wasn't my goal?"

– "It isn't. But it doesn't mean you should not facilitate it when you have the opportunity! Everything is connected: a larger brand awareness makes your job as sales much easier. People have heard of you already, they are in the second section of your sales funnel. While you should focus on obtaining more leads, do not ignore any other positive aspect if you can enforce it."

– "Understood. So what should I be doing now?"

– "Andrew, stop expecting answers to come from the sky and start thinking on your own! You want to drive traffic, so what should you be doing right now?"

I try to hide my frustration and keep my voice steady.

– "I…"

– "Figure it out and call me back once you have the answer."

Seriously? How am I supposed to get this right without any help? Does Charles really understand how critical my situation is?

I spend the rest of the afternoon thinking about how I could drive more traffic and how that would relate to me making an announcement.

Using the meeting room's whiteboard, I start to draw the different pools of people that might come to the event and those I could potentially reach outside the event.

After a while, I end up with an interesting list: customers, partners, suppliers, investors, media, fans and followers and people on our marketing lists. All of them could be reached through one of the following channels: over email contact, Social Media and EDM (Email Direct Marketing).

That's it! I am going to announce our participation so that as many people as possible could come and visit us.

I sit down with Karen and start telling her about my idea. Quickly, she explains me the best way to inform people is to have a uniform cross-channel message. When she realizes she already lost me, she explains:

– "You want to inform as many people as possible about your event but you do not want to spend your budget on a PR announcement. Here is what you should do: start by changing everyone's signature. Have a banner in our team's email signature that announces our participation and booth number. Each time our staff sends an email the recipient is informed of our participation. Do the same with our website and Social Media channels. Soon enough, everyone will know." It seems pretty easy and logical. Why didn't I think of it myself?

– "Alright. That sounds like a good idea. What of the rest? What else should I organize before the event?"

– "There are quite a few important items to plan. Have you thought of internet?"

– "Internet? Why would we need internet?"

She rolls her eyes, obviously annoyed to be training a newbie.

– "You might want to read your emails. You may need to show our website, download a brochure, access a video. You should also use it to record your data online. Internet will be very important, don't forget to arrange it!"

– "I've read that the organizer provides free WiFi for all. That should be enough."

She rolls her eyes again.

– "That's a mistake. The free WiFi will be so weak you couldn't do anything. You can either pay the organizer for a private network or arrange your own, using a prepaid 3G SIM card for example."

Karen shows me an article explaining in details why internet could become really helpful at the fair. After reading it, I can't argue anymore and start looking for internet solutions while a large smile shines on Karen's face. No doubt, I will have to learn from scratch.

Chapter 5.
PREPARING MY LEADS COLLECTION

I'm getting better at it! Karen and I have set up a daily meeting and we work quite well as a team.

We've already decided the color of the carpet, the products to display, and started discussing about logistics… everything is going well and my boss seems quite satisfied with the progress.

It has been almost three weeks since our staff sends emails with the new signature I've created and several customers have already told me about their interest in visiting our booth: great!

My next meeting with Karen will start in about 10 minutes and we are supposed to discuss floor plan and decoration: I have absolutely no knowledge in this field so I will certainly end up listening to her and letting her make decisions.

Something troubles me quite a bit though. All these decisions (carpets, design, organization and so on) are great for brand image and brand awareness but it looks like I have lost sight of my initial goal: getting leads, prospects, and converting them into customers.

When Karen arrives in the room she seems quite excited and smiles at me:

— "I've prepared LOTS of references from our past fairs we can use to build the new floor plan! This booth is going to be amazing! It will be the nicest stall we've ever created!" she says with exaggerated enthusiasm.
— "Look Karen… all we've been doing for the past few weeks has been organizing decoration and arrangement… I'd like to take a different direction." I see her expression change rapidly and her smile fade away. I add "Just for today!" hoping I can get her on board with my idea.
— "Alright. What is it you have in mind?" she asks, listlessly.
— "I was wondering… What is it you guys usually use to collect data?" I ask carefully.
— "Collect data? What kind of data you mean?"
— "Visitors information. Do you collect their details to contact them later?"
— "Duh! Of course we do!" she seems upset with my question - was it that obvious? "We have a standard report template that we will print. Each of us at the show will have to fill this report and attach the visitor's business card

to it."

– "Sounds good. And what kind of data do you collect? Name and email?"

Now she looks almost offended. She raises her voice a little and answers defensively:

– "Of course more than that! We record complete name, email, but also company name, phone number, product interest, quality of the lead as well as some complementary information that could help close a future deal".

– "Wow! That is great!" I am not a great actor and I'm sure she knows I am exaggerating to please her but she seems to calm down nonetheless. "And could you walk me through the next step?"

– "What next step?" she asks, genuinely surprised.

– "Well… collecting all that data is great but what do you do with it?"

– "I have no idea." She thinks for a second, looking at the ceiling. "We pass it to your department. I know there's usually an intern or a sales assistant transferring all these written reports into an excel format… then the sales team start following-up on leads, I guess".

I can't believe we are doing all this work and the organizer herself has no idea what happens with the data we've collected! I try not to panic and ask:

– "And how long would this process take?"

Now she looks fairly exasperated:

– "I have no idea! A week? Ten days? How would I know? What are you looking for exactly?!"

– "I am just trying to understand why we spend so much time, money and efforts on a single event… if no-one even follows-up on the leads we have collected."

Her jaw falls and stops in mid-air for a second or so. Its seems for once I got a good point and she doesn't find anything to respond.

She starts shaking her head and says defensively:

– "Look, these events are mostly for brand awareness. What matters is that people find us, see us, remember us, right? Indeed, it would be great if we could be more efficient at following-up but that's not…"

I'm getting more confident and cut her straight away:

– "I don't think brand awareness is our goal this time."

– "Brand awareness is ALWAYS our goal." she claims, disdainful.

– "Not this time" I say firmly. For the first time since I am in charge, I am SURE to be right. She seems taken aback, obviously unused to me making bold statements. After a few seconds she retorts:

– "Alright Mister Expert. What's our goal then?"

– "Look, you are expert in events organization and I have zero experience. Yet, the boss decided to put ME in charge. Why do you think that is?"

– "I am very busy recently so…"

– "So am I" I say immediately. "Ever since I took this project, I haven't been able to complete my daily tasks once. The reason he put me in charge this time is because he wants it to be SALES oriented. We need to change our goal and aim for sales".

– "You don't sell at a trade show. At a consumer fair you would, but not in a trade exhibition."

– "You are right. I am not talking about selling at the event. I am talking about creating a process that helps us on each level – before, during, after – to achieve our ultimate goal: sell more. I am talking about attracting visitors to our booth. I am talking about collecting prospects information. I am talking about following-up on leads. All these with one unique objective in mind: selling more, acquiring new customers, making business!"

That must be the first time I've talked for that long and Karen doesn't seem used to it. It takes her a couple of seconds to digest my message before answering.

– "We have such process already! I told you: we print reports and…"

– "Obviously that process isn't optimal. Look, don't take it the wrong way, but if you don't even know whether the leads are followed-through, there's something wrong about it."

She swallows slowly and calmly asks:

– "Ok. What do you suggest we do then?"

– "First of all, a week to 10 days to transfer prospects information from written forms to digital doesn't make any sense. How long do you think these prospects remember us? Two? Three days? Four at most? And we are unable to do a follow-up before AT LEAST a week has passed. That can't be! When they finally receive an email from us they probably don't even remember meeting with us in the first place! We must find a way to shorten the process. Maybe hiring more interns after the fair?"

– "There is a pretty large cost involved in the operation. Plus, it wouldn't solve the major issue: most of the time things get delayed because the assistant can't read what the person has been writing. No, that's not the way to go."

Now she's on board. She is with me, trying to find a real solution. She thinks for a while, completely ignoring me, then says: "What about going fully digital this time?"

– "What do you mean?" I ask, curious and excited about her going in my direction.

– "Well, instead of recording things with pen and paper, we record it all digitally from the beginning! That way the data is ready immediately after the event and we avoid not only delays but also human error!"

– "That's genius!" I say genuinely excited. "Any idea how we can achieve that?"

– "I've heard of a system that can do that: it works on smartphone, tablet or laptop and is made specifically for this purpose. It records visitors information, takes photos, add tags…"

– "That's EXACTLY what we need! That closes my loop!"

– "Your 'loop'? What loop are you talking about?"

– "I have been talking with an event expert and he told me I need to find my goal – acquiring customers and selling in our case – and define a strategy for each of the three steps – before, during, after – in order to achieve that goal.

I believe that's what we've just done! FIRST we drive traffic to our booth – we achieve that with the announcement and with the stall design. SECOND, we record visitors information directly from our stall – we will make that much more efficient by giving up the pen & paper strategy and using a digital tool. THIRD, we follow-up with prospects and make sure we don't let them forget us! I haven't figured this step yet, but I know my objective."

She now seems as excited as I am but can't help to reply: – "An event expert? No wonder you became so smart suddenly…". I look at her, trying to see if she's being serious. After a few seconds she starts laughing and I happily follow along.

It's now 10pm and I think it is time for me to call Charles and let him know of my progress. After I tell him the story, he replies:
– "Well done Andrew! You are right on track now! And you've even figured out your major bottleneck."
– "My 'bottleneck'? What do you mean?"
– "Pen and paper! Most exhibitorsat trade shows still use pen and paper! It is slow, unreadable, leads to delay and human errors, not to mention the ecological aspect of it… Removing this steps will increase your efficiency a LOT!"
– "Well… thanks. Now I need to look into digital solutions. You have any to recommend?"
– "You have to spend some time analyzing and comparing

solutions. You must find one that truly fits your requirements. Something that will help you record visitors information, add tags and comments, take some photos, send instant thank you emails, and so on."

– "Great! Thank you so much Charles!"

Things are seeming to go well now. For the first time in a few weeks, I will sleep like a baby tonight.

Chapter 6.
MY FIRST FLOOR PLAN

We have two hours to prepare before the weekly meeting with the boss. Karen and I are both very excited about it and arrived quite early to the office this morning. When she sees me, Karen runs to my desk.

– "I found the perfect tool! I know how we can collect data at the exhibition! " She takes a peek at my screen and realizes that I am already looking at it.
– "I've just finished checking out their website." She looks a little disappointed for a second that I've wasted her initial enthusiasm but quickly smiles again.
– "So how does it look? Can we use it for our fair?"
– "Yes, seems pretty great. But we need to set it up first."
– "Set it up? How do you mean?"
– "Upload our logo, complete our profile and so on…"
– "I can take care of that!"
– "And we can set up tags to categorize visitors and prepare emails templates… I'll handle that part."

– "Perfect! Now it's time to discuss floor plan!"
– "Floor plan? What is that? "

For over an hour, Karen walks me through drawings and pictures of tons of booths she takes as reference. I can't help but yawn. It seems she has noticed it from the corner of her eye: she stops immediately and says:
– "Ok, enough references for the time being. Now we need to prepare our own!"
– "What do you mean?"
– "We know the booth location and size, right?"
– "Right" I say. "And then?"
– "Now is time to define what we put where! Did you expect all these things would just magically appear?"
– "I guess not… I didn't think about it actually."
– "It's about time! We have a list of products we want to display. First, we need to see how to regroup them, then we will have to see what furniture we need to display them. Afterwards, we will study how to arrange the furniture so that everything fits on the stall and we will start talking about posters and wall decoration!" She seems incredibly excited about it. I can't say the same for myself.
– "Hey Karen… you seem to be quite an expert in this field. What about you handle that part and we discuss it again once you've decided the details?"
– "Alright!" she says with a big smile before running out of the meeting room, her hands full of documents and papers.

– "Andrew, how is the project going? The Electronics Show is getting closer and closer, is everything on track?"

– "Sure is, boss!" I say, pretty confident.

– "Glad to hear that. So, how many promoters did you hire?"

– "Promoters…? What promoters?"

He puts his head in his hands. The whole room gets awfully silent for a few seconds. Karen and I exchange a worried look.

– "Karen! Your job is to help Andrew leading this project, right?"

– "Right" she says with a very low voice. She is obviously very uncomfortable and expects a storm to start anytime.

– "Then WHY have you guys not started to take care of promoters?!"

My boss is in his late forties, early fifties. 1.8m high, maybe 1.85. He has large shoulders and looks like he could destroy the room with his bare hands. I've never seen him angry but I've heard stories about it. I'm not sure I would ever want to experience this myself. He now has a blue vein on his forehead. It seems pretty obvious he is about to explode. If I do nothing, Karen is going to have a very hard time in the coming seconds.

– "We will arrange promoters right after this meeting" I say. I see he is about to reply, so I continue to avoid whatever's coming. "And we have found a new method to improve our results in the booth!"

It seems I managed to trigger his interest. He looks at me

for a second, judging me, then says calmly:

– "Good. What is it?"

While looking at him I can see Karen in a corner having a long sigh of relief. I think she might owe me one now!

– "That's an online system. It will help us collect data digitally."

He looks very suspicious. He is obviously not convinced but seems willing to give me a chance to explain. He asks:

– "We have always used pen & paper and it has worked pretty well for us. How is your solution any better?"

– "First we will reduce the risk of human errors by recording it all once only instead of twice." He doesn't buy it. "Also, it will enable us to take photos and add tags to make the whole report more useful".

My boss obviously isn't tech savvy. He has used the same techniques for the past 20 years and isn't keen to change them. Before he has a chance to reply, I add:

– "Most of all, it will save us lots of money!" I see his eyebrows move and I know I now have his full attention. "With this system, we no longer need to hire part timers to transfer the data from paper to excel. Also, we will reduce considerably the gap between the event and the follow-up, increasing our chances to convert leads into customers!"

He considers my suggestion for a few seconds then approves it. Karen presents the details we've discussed and the rest of the meeting goes smoothly.

3pm: I need to call Charles to let him know I got my boss to approve the use of digital solutions!

– "Glad you could convince him, it's not always that easy."
– "And I also managed to free myself a lot of extra time to focus on this project. I've passed the whole 'floor-plan-thingy' to my colleague" I say, quite proud of myself.
– "You WHAT?" says Charles, panicked. "You CANNOT outsource this part!"
– "Why? This is just marketing. I focus on sales, remember? I leave to her the marketing and I get the sales strategy. Isn't it what you said?"
– "Yes, but the floor plan isn't exclusively for marketing! You have lots of details to manage there!"
It feels like my energy is being drained out of my body. All the motivation I have built today has suddenly vanished. Empty, ashamed, I slowly ask with a small voice:
– "What exactly do you have in mind?"
– "Well, the flow to start with! Your marketing team will try to put multiple messages, lots of products and furniture… They will end up obstructing the way and disturbing the flow of visitors. You also need to choose the place you need to have TVs for demonstrations. You must consider having a welcome desk to distribute flyers and business cards while driving visitors in your stall. You should also construct a small cabin to help storing your water and cleaning items. You have lots to prepare and you can't trust someone else with this!"

Charles and I keep talking for a while. I take notes like a good student, I carefully listen to all details. After an hour, Charles finally manages to hang up and leave me with a million other questions.

It had been such a great day, too bad it had to end that way. Tonight I can't seem to fall asleep. I keep thinking about blueprints, cleaning products and other elements mentioned by Charles. I will need to have a long discussion with Karen tomorrow...

Chapter 7.
ALL THE SMALL DETAILS

– "Look, this is not about trust. It has NOTHING to do with trust. I trust you a hundred percent!"

– "Then what is it all about?!" replies Karen, outraged.

– "I just want to get involved to make sure we are on the same page, that's it." I try to temper my response. "Could you just show me your floor plan so that we could discuss it?"

– "Alright" she says unconvinced. "Here you go. So that is the top view, here you have the entrance and there…" I am horrified by what I see and I don't do a great job hiding it. "WHAT?!" she asks impatiently.

If she would have shown me her floor plan yesterday, I would certainly have found it perfect. But after so much time with Charles over the phone my perspective has shifted.

– "Just… I am surprised to see that you closed the second entrance…"

– "That is to maximize the available display space and add

more visuals and messages."

– "And this table here in the entrance?" I ask calmly.

– "A reception desk, can't you see it?" she replies, annoyed.

– "Look Karen, don't take it the wrong way, but that's not at all what I envisioned." She opens her mouth to replicate but I continue without letting her a chance to stop me. "That LOOKS fabulous. Really! Design-wise, it is great and attractive. But I think our objectives are just not aligned. Can we take one step back to discuss the purpose of this booth?"

My request must have been somehow reasonable because she complies, breathes deeply and gets ready to discuss.

– "We agreed on the fact that the objective of our presence at this trade show was to increase our business volume. Right?", she nods. "Ok. Now, to achieve that, we have also agreed on the fact that we need to follow-up exhibitions leads coming from proper prospects and capturedetails at the booth. Correct?", she nods again.

I use a technique suggested by Charles that appears to be very efficient: when facing a disagreement with a person, go back to the root of the problem and escalate point by point, reconfirming basics that both parties agreed on. If you follow this process well enough, in the worst case you will be able to identify where your visions start to divert, in the best case you will just erase the problem and get the other to agree with you.

– "Now, if I continue with the same logic, in order for us to maximize the leads collection, we need to maximize the traffic to our booth as well, right?"

– "Yes! And that is exactly why I want to install very large advertising panels all around the booth to increase visibility!" she says offensively. I remain calm.

– "The problem is that your system blocks most of the flow." She wants to reply but I keep going. "We need to balance our efforts. An empty booth would be great to walk around but wouldn't attract anyone. An over-branded booth might be appealing but this appeal would be wasted if no-one could visit it, right?" she nods slightly. "Do you remember why we picked this booth location in the first place?"

– "Because it was in the right section, on a large alley."

– "And also…?"

– "Because it was at the end of the aisle… and it has two open sides." she admits unwillingly, starting to see where I am heading.

– "Exactly! With a booth that has two open sides you multiply your accessibility and increase your potential traffic! But if you close one side with a banner and the other with a large reception desk, you waste this initial benefit."

I can see she agrees but hates it. However, since she doesn't object, I continue.

– " I suggest that we remove this panel and open the booth on that side. As for the reception desk, that's a brilliant idea:

great location for a large logo, to hold some flyers and business cards and direct visitors to the right product. But we need to reduce its size by at least 50%".

Karen does not reply anymore. It seems I have been able to convince her. I'm a pretty good salesperson after all!

I can feel Karen needs to take a break. She has been leading the organization of all events for a few years already and having to negotiate with a newbie like me isn't exactly her cup of tea. We decide to continue this discussion later today.

At 5 pm, when Karen and I sit down again, I have had time to go through my notes from last night's conversation with Charles. There are a couple more points I want to touch and I am sure that will not be easy.

Karen is already in the room, waiting for me, looking at a few plans left on the table. When she sees me approaching she greets me with a large smile:
– "Hello Andrew! Glad we could continue this discussion!"
She obviously had time to recharge her battery – she's now full of energy and ready to battle.
– "I have revised all the plans based on our discussion this morning and I think you will love the new design!"
While I am quite happy to see her motivated and positive again, I was not planning for a new floor plan so soon. I have a few more changes I want to bring up and I feel like

it will contradict her strategy.

I don't even have time to properly sit on my chair that she already starts explaining her concept.

Fifteen minutes later, she has presented – almost – all the new elements. There is only one thing I don't understand. A rectangle in the booth' corner is placed exactly where I would need some extra space for my idea.

– "And this one here, in the corner… what is it?"

She must have been waiting for me to ask this question for a long time. She looks absolutely delighted when she answers me.

– "This is my best idea!" she says. "That, my dear, is a sofa!" seeing me surprised, she explains: "We want people to stay longer in our booth, right? A sofa will achieve that! Take a comfortable seat and have a long conversation with visitors… then transform them into customers!"

Karen seems so excited and proud of her idea. I don't know how to bring up the fact that it might not be that great after all. Hesitantly, I say:

– "This sounds great, really!"

– "But?" she asks, frowning and expecting my reaction.

– "But… while I think having a sofa is really a good idea, there might be some better use of that space."

– "Like what?" she replies, a bit aggressive.

– "Like a cabin."

– "A cabin? What do you need it for? Planning on playing hide and seek?"

– "Haha" I laugh nervously, "no, actually, a small cabin

could be a real asset. Think about it: a place to rest, to store our products, some water, cleaning products…"

I expect a negative reaction from Karen. She thinks for a while and replies:

– "Not a bad idea!" with a smile. "You're getting better and better at this!"

– "Well… Actually… that's more like Charles' suggestion"

– "I guessed. That's too smart to be your idea!" she teases me.

We both laugh and continue the meeting positively, fine-tuning the last few details needed for the event organization.

Chapter 8.
LET'S TALK STATISTICS

As I arrive in the office this morning I feel confident. I have been looking at the plan all night and it really feels perfect.

I am a little early and decide to sit in the meeting room for a while and review the plans one last time before presenting it to our boss later today.
When I open the door, Karen is already there with papers all over the table.

– "Morning Karen! How are you doing?" She jumps, obviously not expecting anyone to be around.
– "Hi Andrew! I've been studying."
– "So I see! Do you mind telling me what kind of study brought you here this early?"
– "Remember why it was decided that YOU should be in charge of this event?"
– "Yes… to take a sales approach instead of the usual

marketing approach for exhibitions." I don't really see where she's heading.

– "Right. So I've been studying, trying to find strategies and statistics to see how we could benefit from this approach."

I am quite impressed with her continual grit and enthusiasm. Now that I think about it, Karen is still very young – probably a couple of years older than me – yet she is leading our marketing efforts. No doubt her persistence helped her climb the professional ladder faster than most.

– "Alright, so what have you found?"

– "I read a very interesting article from 'exhibitor online'. Did you know that 98% of exhibitors collect leads at fairs and trade shows?"

It appears quite obvious to me: why would you pay such insane price for a single event if you couldn't get proper leads for future business? Apparently, Karen is part of the remaining 2% that consider it more like a marketing event for brand awareness.

– "Oh really?" I say, trying hard to appear genuine. But Karen is so focused on her findings that she does not even notice my poor acting and continues:

– "Also, 70% of exhibitors have a follow-up plan BEFORE the event."

This one is more surprising.

– "What do you mean a 'follow-up plan'?"

– "They don't explain that part… but I expect they have answers to the basic question: who, when, how?"

I am trying to visualize what a follow-up plan could be.

Who? When? How? Isn't it obvious? Who is us, when is after the event and how… well… by email, I guess. I'm lost in my thoughts when Karen suddenly brings me back to earth:

– "Also, 85% of exhibitors take more than 48h to start following-through with their collected leads. Some of them don't event follow-up at all!"

– "Hold on… You mean that less than 15% of exhibitors actually perform immediate or quick follow-up?"

– "Exactly!"

– "You know what that means?" Karen looks puzzled. "That means that if we manage to send follow-up messages within 48h we will be faster than 85% of our competitors! That would give us a real strategic advantage over the others! That is the kind of edge that can help us get more business and turn this event into a huge success!"

– "But I am not sure how we could perform that… there is a reason why most people take over 48 hours: it is because it is close to impossible to be faster!"

– "Well… your system, the one we signed for."

– "You mean our lead capture solution?"

– "Exactly. This tool will help us collect data digitally AND send instant "thank-you-for-visiting-us" emails, right?" Karen nods.

– "Then the problem is solved! We will have instant follow-up and someone will send them a second email later in-case they wouldn't have replied us."

– "And who would be 'someone'?"

– "Right… I don't know… an intern maybe?"

– "According to the survey, 37% of the leads are followed-up by sales, 33% by marketing and the rest is usually handled by various other departments."

– "Alright then. We'll divide the workload: 50% on me, 50% on you! Now let's rehearse, we have a meeting with the boss this afternoon and I'd like it to go well!"

The discussion with our boss goes fairly well. He has some things to comment on but, overall, it is a success. It is now 8pm and I want to call Charles to let him know about my progress.

– "Hello Charles! Am I disturbing?"

– "Hi Andrew. No you're not. How is the organization of your event going?"

I start telling him about the floor plan, the cabin, Karen's idea about the sofa and so on. After I'm done talking about the statistics discovered by my marketing colleague, Charles asks me:

– "Very good findings indeed! So what will you do about it?"

– "What do you mean?"

– "Now you know that 70% of exhibitors have a follow-up plan, what are you going to do with this piece of information?"

– "Well… Build a follow-up plan I guess, but I already have one."

– "Oh really?" he replies amused, "And what is your plan?"

– "I will capture visitors information and send instant follow-up emails using templates I have pre-written. We will be using this system we discussed last time."

– "Andrew, that is not a plan. This is not even a follow-up!"

– "What do you mean?"

– "Sending instant emails is brilliant. You will make sure your visitors remember you longer and you have the opportunity to thank them for their visit. It is great. But it isn't a follow-up. Follow-ups are deeper communications and require a different approach for each visitor." Charles stops for a second. It seems he is trying to give me time to digest this part before attacking the next one. "Send these instant emails, perfect. But once back to the office, export all visitors reports and follow-up one by one."

– "Who? Me? Can't we do 50/50 with marketing?"

– "Oh Andrew…" he sounds despaired, like if he couldn't believe what I just asked. "There is no 50/50, we are not playing lottery here! Qualify your leads: hot, warm, cold. Give absolute priority to the hot leads and review them personally. For the warm ones, you can eventually pass them to another sales person, but don't delay too much! 72h max!"

– "And the cold ones?" I ask.

– "The cold ones can go to marketing. They can follow-up with more generic emails and offers. There is a reason why you qualified them as cold: they are too high in the sales funnel with low chances of conversion. Pass them to marketing to push them down your sales funnel - that is called lead-nurturing. Once they're fully grown, you could re-attack personally!"

– "Wow… How did I not think of that? It sounds obvious when you mention it…"

– "Talking about obvious… how are you planning on following up? Which channel will you use?"

– "Email of course"

– "Emails are great because they are fast, you can think of what to write and attach files. But hand-written notes and phone calls can be very effective too!"

– "How do you decide?"

– "All 'normal' leads can receive emails only. Those you know will be difficult, follow-up with a phone call as well to clarify details and push a little more. And for these customers that represent BIG contracts, take a few minutes for an additional hand written note. That shows you care. Business is all about trust and care. Use it!"

– "Thank you so much Charles!"

Chapter 9.
WHAT ABOUT PROMOTERS

It is 4 o'clock in the morning when I wake up, panicked, realizing I still haven't arranged any promoter for our booth. I'm not even sure to know where to find promoters or what they are supposed to help me with.

I am pretty certain calling Charles at this early hour wouldn't be a smart idea but going back to bed is out of the question. I decide to send a message to Karen and start looking for information on the internet.

"Hi Karen! Do you remember our conversation about promoters? I think we need to hire some ASAP!"

I just have time to press my laptop's power button before my phone vibrates on the table. I grab it and look. The screen displays "Don't worry, I've arranged it already!"Does she actually EVER sleep? Karen seems to be as efficient at night as she is in the daytime.

Now that I am fully awake and my computer is turned on, I

decide it isn't worth going back to sleep and will instead make myself some coffee to help me during my research: "what are promoters supposed to do in a trade show booth?"

I browse a bunch of articles talking about promoters and hostesses in exhibition stalls and the more I read the more confused I get... are they fully part of the booth-staff? Are they just here to distribute flyers? Are hostesses only supposed to be sexy-and-smiling young ladies driving traffic to our sales team? It seems everyone has its own opinion as for what promoters & hostesses are supposed to achieve at an exhibition.

As I scratch my head after reading another article I look at my watch: 8.45am! I am really late! I send myself some articles via email, jump into a pair of trousers, brush my teeth in a hurry and run out of my apartment.

As I enter the bus, I open my emails on my smartphone and start browsing a few more articles – I takes about 15 minutes to reach the office and I should be able to read a bit more before work.

– "TERMINUS!"
I open my eyes. Where am I? I look around me searching for something I could recognize.
– "That's the last stop young man!" says the driver, impatient.
I am still in the bus! My watch shows 9.45am and I am

nowhere close to the office. I check my phone that slipped from my fingers to the floor – 4 missed calls. I storm out of the bus, hail a cab and send it straight to the office while dialing on my phone.

– "Hi Karen! Look, I'm sorry but…"

– "Where have you been?? I called you four times!"

– "I know, I was…"

– "No time for that, there's an emergency here! I've received a call from the part-time staff agency I always work with and the two hostesses I hired earlier bailed on us! And you can be sure the boss will ask about it, we need to come up with a backup plan right away!"

– "I'll be in the office in ten".

When I finally arrive it is past 10 o'clock. Lucky for me, my boss is not around – I won't have to go through a long explanation. Karen seems incredibly panicked. When she sees me coming she runs towards me and drags me in the meeting room.

– "I can't believe you text me at 4am but then manage to be late for work!" as I open my mouth to reply she waves her hand to keep me quiet and continues "Ok, we need to find promoters now! So I need you to help me make a few phone calls".

– "Karen, I have a question." I hesitate for a second but as she looks at me impatiently I decide to ask "What do we need promoters for?"

Karen's eyes widen, trying to evaluate whether I am making fun of her or being serious. She finally decides to ignore my question and say "We don't have time for that, let's fix this problem first!"

With a sudden excess of confidence, I catch her arms as she turns back.

– "Look, Karen, we have to figure out WHY we are hiring promoters if we want it to be efficient."

– "Are you serious?! We need promoters to P-R-O-M-O-T-E our booth! Is it really that complicated?"

Keeping my calm, I reply:

– "And what does 'promote' mean? What do you ACTUALLY expect from these promoters?". I think Karen has been organizing so many events in the past using the same method she never took the time to think about WHY she was doing what she was doing.

– "We want pretty girls distributing flyers, attracting people and directing them to our booth and making demos to visitors. As simple as this."

– "Is it the right strategy? I mean… I understand that is what we have always done, but since we are changing strategy quite a bit this time, wouldn't it be worth finding out what we really expect from promoters also?"

After two hours of discussion, Karen and I have made a list of things promoters and hostesses can potentially help with:

- driving traffic to the booth
- distributing flyers
- welcoming visitors
- giving demonstrations

- capturing leads

We decide to ignore our traditional methods – if we are to hire someone, that person should be doing more than just smile or distribute pamphlets. Our promoters will be treated as any other sales person at the booth – that means we need to train them. With the help of some interesting articles discussing various aspects of hiring and managing hostesses and part-timers, we set out to build a clear plan.

When the boss finally shows up around 3pm, we are both smiling and confident with a clear idea of our promoter strategy. It seems I will sleep better tonight than yesterday!

Chapter 10.
SETTING UP A TRAINING SESSION

I haven't called Charles for a few days already. I think I am now able to manage things on my own – no need to disturb him unnecessarily. I am starting to really feel "in charge" and I am more confident each day.

I have decided to manage the whole training process on my own. I have informed Karen she would not need to worry about this part – this is being handled!

When I arrive in the office this morning I lock myself in the small meeting room, steal the white board and a few pens and start preparing my plan.

When I get out, two hours later, I have figured everything out. I invite Karen to join me as I reveal my plan:

– "We must invite our 3 part-time promoters to come to our office 2 weeks before the event. We will organize a three hours training for demonstration – what are the benefits of the product, how it works, what are the specs, and so on". I show a complete demonstration plan to Karen and spend 20 minutes explaining it in details then I stop a few seconds to leave Karen a chance to jump in.

– "Wow, that's great… But you are aware of the fact that you actually need to PAY these promoters to come to training?"

– "I sure do! But think about it: we will spend a couple hundred more… and get much more leads from the event! Isn't it worth it?"

– "Probably' she says, still thinking. I don't give her sufficient time to give more feedback and say:

– "Then it is done!" and I leave the room, full of vim and vigor.

When I leave the office I cannot resist the temptation to show off a little with Charles. I dial his number, rehearsing my perfect speech in my head.

– "What?!" he says when picking up my call. He is obviously not in a good day and I instantly lose all confidence.

– "Hi Charles, it's Andrew… hope I'm not calling at the wrong time…"

– "No, that's fine" he says, sounding impatient. "What's going on Andrew?"

– "Just wanted to catch up with you… to make sure I keep you in the loop and let you know what's going on with my side."

He doesn't respond. I decide to keep going.

– "I have hired a few promoters this week. One promoter and two hostesses to be precise."
– "And?"
– "And..." his short temper increases the pressure on my shoulders, making it difficult to organize my thoughts. "And I've prepared an action plan for their training!"
– "Glad to hear that Andrew!" he says somehow enthusiastic. "Tell me more, what will your training be like?"
I quickly regain confidence as he shows interest and reply:
– "I will spend two hours with them showing them how to perform a demonstration!" I say proudly.
– "And...?" replies Andrew, waiting for more details.
– "Well... that's it. We will show them the product, how it works, talk about USP, features, benefits..."
– "Do you really believe that could be enough?" I feel like a black hole in my stomach absorbing everything around. "Can you remind me your goal? Why are you participating in this event?"
– "To get extra business..."
– "Come on Andrew, let's not go through this again!" he says, obviously exasperated. "How do you plan on achieving that?!" All traces of confidence and pride vanish from my mind. I am completely depressed and scared. Quickly, I think of an answer and reply:
– "I plan on getting more business by converting prospects

into customers. I will get these prospects from leads captured in my booth through discussions with visitors."
– "Great! Great, Andrew. That's exactly it!" I give a hint of a smile... not that bad after all! But he doesn't give up:
– "So what should your promoters help you with? What crucial element do you need to teach them?"
I hesitate and finally decide to answer:
– "Taking notes to help me capturing leads?" I say shyly.
– "Don't you think it would be a giant waste of resources to hire someone to take notes on your behalf at an exhibition when there are so many other things he could help with? Think Andrew, think!"
– "I guess he could help capturing leads by himself..."
– "Right! That's it! Exactly! You got it!" he says with apparent relief. I must admit I am quite relieved myself. He keeps going: "You must train your promoters and hostesses, not to smile or take notes like robots, but to be your brand ambassadors. That means promoting your brand, presenting your product, explaining its features, but also..." I cut him to end his sentence I believe I could predict:
– "... recognizing a good lead and capturing it!"
– "You are right! So what should your next move be?"
– "I will interview each of them... define who's got the best potential and train them."
– "And what should you train them on?"
– "There shall be one section about the company's history, mission and vision... one section about the products features and benefits as well as demonstration... and one

part about questions to ask and information to collect once the lead qualified."

– "All clear Andrew, good job! But do you know yet how to qualify a good lead yourself?"

I have read a **good article** about it lately and I am pretty convinced I could differentiate a good lead from a bad one. It is all about having an efficient qualifying process where we ask visitors relevant questions in order to identify their profile and potential before devoting too much time or presenting irrelevant products.

– "Sure! It is all a matter of asking the right questions, I can do that!"

– "Great then! I've got to go Andrew, I have quite a few problems of my own to deal with".

Before I have a chance to thank him, Charles has already hung up. Now, I need to swallow my pride and tell Karen my initial idea was bad… It feels like tomorrow won't be an easy day.

When Karen arrives in the office, she sees me staring at the whiteboard and wave at me:

– "Hi Andrew! Early bird, ah? What's going on?" she says with a smile.

– "Just reviewing my plan… I've been thinking about it and… 2 hours training might not be enough after all…"

– "Someone talked with Charles last night" she teases me with a large smile. I can feel my face getting red and decide not to reply.

– "So I'm thinking we should organize a screening first – find out who would be the best candidates for this job then interview them".

– "You want to screen and interview promoters… to distribute flyers?" she replies, skeptical.

– "Not distribute flyers. I want them to be part of the team and help us sell!"

– "But… that's not something you learn in a few minutes! It took years for our team to figure out how to sell, and you expect newbies to catch up instantly?"

– "No, of course. I expect them to assist us the best they could and pass us the leads when things get too complicated. Here is my idea: first week we advertise the jobs and screen applications. Second week we do group interviews to speed up the process. Third week we identify the best candidates and bring them in for a training."

– "Alright… what would that training be all about?"

– "I'm glad you ask!" I say smiling.

For the rest of the morning, I explain my training plan in details.

– "So, what do you think Karen?"

– "Pretty great… but I'm getting hungry! Let's do lunch".

Karen and I go to a Dim Sum place – a traditional Chinese restaurant popular for family brunches and team lunches. When opening the office door to go to the restaurant, our boss catches us:

– "You guys going for lunch?"
– "Yes, we are going to the Dim Sum place nearby… there are still a few things we want to review regarding the booth promoters training"
– "Perfect, I come with you!"

I look at Karen – why did I let her talk? Our relaxing lunch is now turning into a stressful meeting.

Chapter 11.
THE RIGHT BOOTH APPROACH

– "So what's the plan?" asks my boss while swallowing a giant piece of Cha Siu Bao, a white bun filled with barbecue pork.

– "We are inviting all the candidates that passed our screening process for a group interview session next week".

– "Group interview? What kind of questions will you ask?" he asks while rushing down some other dumplings.

– "We will start with a short company introduction and product demonstration. Then we will give them a questionnaire to fill with questions related to our company and products, to test their memory and interest. We will keep the best ones and go through a group workshop."

– "What kind of workshop?" he keeps asking questions and jumps on the spring rolls while I answer. If it keeps going that way I won't have eaten anything by the end of this meal.

– "Karen and I will play a visitor / booth staff conversation. I will highlight the different stages of the talk: opening question, qualifying questions, product demonstration, USPs highlight, next steps discussion and conversation ending."

He stops eating for a minute to look at me:
– "You don't talk about data recording?"
– "Not at this stage" I reply confidently. "For the moment we want to discover who has the best potential. Since we are not planning on keeping everyone, there is no reason to reveal all our strategies. We will discuss data recording with those that pass this step."
He looks very satisfied with my answer. I must say I've grown a lot in the past few weeks. As complicated as it feels, this project has truly helped me develop new skills and improve my organization and presentation abilities. I should probably give a call to Charles tonight, just to thank him for his tremendous help.
– "Alright Andrew, keep going. What is the 'opening question' you mentioned earlier?"
Karen must have noticed that I didn't touch the food yet and that there is almost nothing left. With a smile she answers the question for me while I reach for some Siu Long Bao – some kind of pork dumpling filled with hot soup that you dip in black vinegar. It would have been delicious if only it was still hot.
– "The traditional way for people to greet visitors on their booth is with 'Hello', 'Welcome', 'How are you?', and so on." Karen explains.
– "True. And?"
– "And while this might seem to be the right approach

because it is nice and polite, it doesn't engage any conversation. What do you reply to 'Hello' besides 'Hello'?"

– "I see… keep going.". He stopped eating. I think Karen found the right strategy to trigger his interest. I decide not to waste this opportunity and attack the next dish that originally looked delicious but now looks half-finished.

– "Instead, we train our promoters to use 'open questions' to greet visitors. 'What brings you here today?', 'What company do you work for?', 'What are you looking for exactly?', 'What product do you currently use?', 'What are the challenges with your current product?', etc. Such question will force the visitor to give a longer more articulated answer that will engage a proper conversation."

– "Smart… you not only get the conversation going but you also start gathering information… I like that!".

Karen smiles and continues:
– "Then, traditionally, we should continue with a product demonstration."
– "Of course."
– "But not this time." Karen stops here, obviously trying to trigger the question she expected:
– "And why is that?" Karen smiles, satisfied things go as planned.
– "When you talk, you are only repeating what you already know. But if you listen, you may learn something new. Do you know this quote from the Dalai Lama?"
– "Maybe…" my boss says, chewing on some dumpling.
– "Well, that's the idea. Instead of trying to talk and present

as much as we can, the strategy will be to understand the needs and problems of the visitors. Only then, we would present the product they might need and focus on this one only. Less talk, more listening – that way we provide the right solutions and increase our selling probabilities."

– "Sounds… reasonable." he says, thinking. "But then you might miss opportunities of selling more."

– "Not really. Instead of trying to sell things people might not need, we present ONLY what people are looking for. Then, we focus on providing not a full list of USPs, but the ones that we know will convince people because we already assessed their needs and problems."

– "Alright, you got me on board with that strategy! Good job guys, well done!"

I decide to jump back in now that I've had a chance to eat a bit.

– "That's not all. We've also identified 'qualifying questions'."

– "What is that?" my boss asks, genuinely surprised. Satisfied, I continue:

– "A set of questions we will get the team to memorize that will help qualifying the leads." Because he looks puzzled, I decide to go further in my explanation. "I expect we will meet a ton of people at that event. Therefore, we will get lots of leads and it will surely take time to follow-up each one of them carefully. But the truth is, not all leads have the same value nor carry the same weight. Some of them are just entering our sales funnel while others are almost ready to sign – we must prioritize our leads. And to achieve that, we will be asking qualifying questions".

– "It makes sense… what kind of questions do you have in mind?" he asks.

– "I recently read **an article that** contained lots of smart questions. The idea is to first identify the visitor's profile: is he from the media? Is he a distributor? A competitor? Finding information about the person's company and business is the first step."

– "Ok, I agree. What then?"

– "Then it is about identifying his product usage and knowledge. If he knows WAY too much, that might be a competitor trying to collect information. If he knows nothing, he is most certainly in the early stage of the sales funnel and requires further nurturing and education. That already gives some idea of his potential as a customer."

– "Alright. What comes next?"

– "Once identified, if it sounds like a potential lead, it is time to dig a little deeper. We've prepared a set of questions that will achieve that. Things like: what territories does he cover? Is he a decision maker? How badly does he need the product? Is it a product he already distributes? Does he ask for logistics, payment terms, MOQ, etc.? All these questions help defining how serious is the lead then we can qualify it as 'Hot', 'Warm' or 'Cold' and…"

Karen jumps in:

– "… then while Andrew follows-up closely with hot leads, I will send EDM batches to the cold ones and we will split

the warm leads case-by-case." she says, satisfied.
– "Well… you guys did an amazing job! It seems you are in charge and know your topic! I'm impressed, well done!"

We both smile naturally – it wasn't easy, but we've done it!

– "Ok guys, the bill is on me, let's go back to work – I'm sure you still have a lot to prepare and there isn't much time left!"

Chapter 12.
ASSEMBLING THE PUZZLE

Time flies and there is only one week left before the beginning of the show. I have spent the past two weeks reviewing my budget and expenses, making sure everything was accounted for. I overspent by about 15% – according to Karen, it is unexpectedly reasonable.

I am meeting with Charles this afternoon, in a coffee shop nearby my house. Over the phone, he said he was proud of me and wanted to meet-up to discuss fine-tuning. I am pretty confident things will go smooth this time.

– "Hi Andrew!" Charles is already sitting in a comfortable chair in the back of the shop and waves energetically in my direction. His large smile seems to indicate he is thrilled to see me.
– "Hello Charles! Am I late? Have you been waiting for long?"
– "Nonsense! I was enjoying a delicious cup of macchiato: I did not know they made such great coffee around here!"
– "Yes, it's a very nice place and the environment is quite

relaxing. But… since it is quite pricey I seldom come here…"

– "No worries, today is on ME." claims Charles, obviously excited about it.

– "No Charles, I should be the one to…"

Charles ignores me and goes on following his idea:

– "So, tell me more about your journey! It seems you've evolved quite a bit since the first time you called me! When was it? About 6 months ago?"

– "That's about right…"

– "And when is the event starting?"

– "Next week, actually."

– "Wow, you must be fairly excited about it!" Honestly, right now, Charles is the one who looks all excited. It seems he can't contain himself, admiring the creature he has created.

– "I don't know… maybe. I just hope things will go as planned".

– "Sure it won't! Things NEVER go as planned.". That's reassuring, thank you Charles. "Have you heard of Murphy?"

– "Murphy…? You mean another school mate?"

– "No, Murphy as in 'Murphy's law'! 'Everything that can go wrong will go wrong'. That's a rule, nothing ever goes as planned. That's why you need to always have a plan B! What is yours?"

– "I've got a passport to disappear to Mexico if things don't go to plan…"

– "HAHAHA! Glad to hear that! Not sure a mustache

would fit you though…" Charles is getting quite loud and enthusiastic. People turn around, staring at him but he doesn't seem to notice… or care.

– "Ok, Andrew, time to be a little serious" in the blink of an eye, Charles' attitude completely changed. He is now very focused and ready to talk business. "Tell me, what have you done for the past few days?"
– "I have been working on my expenses sheet." Suddenly regaining confidence, I puff out my chest and claim "I am only 15% over budget, this is the best score our company ever had!".
Charles stares at me, studying me carefully. My smile slowly fades away – he is apparently not as proud as I am and there must be something wrong with what I said.
– "15% over, you consider it a good score? Let me ask you something: when did you start managing your expenses?"
– "A couple of weeks ago…"
– "That is late. WAY too late." says Andrew, shaking his head slowly looking at me in despair. "Look, what is done is done, but here is what you should have done: from day 1, have a checklist ready. This list should contain everything – booth rental, TVs, samples, carpets, lighting, hotels, logistics, etc. Then, you should allocate your budget based on how you wish to spend it. Last, as you organize the event, you should update this sheet with actual expenses. That's the way to go to not overspend."
– "Yes… I have seen that the tool we use to help us organize the event, provides such feature… I just did not think it would matter so much until recently." Charles and I

are about the same age and we've studied together. Yet, it feels like he is now my teacher and I must report to him. How did that happen?

I must have been lost in my thoughts since Charles had to bring me back to earth:
– "Andrew! Are you still with me?"
– "Yes, yes, sorry, I was thinking about this budgeting thing…"
– "Well, that is now behind you, let's focus on what you can still improve. Let's talk about your tool box. Have you prepared one yet?"
– "Tool…box… I am not sure to know what you mean."
– "I have prepared this article for you" Charles reaches out to his inside pocket an extracts an A4 printed sheet that he passes me. "It contains tips about what a proper trade show toolbox should contain. Please do NOT go to the exhibition without it, that would be a huge mistake!"
I look at the article: "**What tools should I prepare for my trade show**" – it looks like there are quite a few details I should organize urgently.

– "The most important items are listed here. Have you prepared some pen, paper, stapler…?"
– "No. We don't need to. We will record all our leads digitally!" I claim with pride.
– "Yes, and that's brilliant and all, but…" he expects me to finish his sentence. Shyly, I say:
– "Murphy's law?"
– "Right! Exactly! What happens if you run out of battery,

your tablet dies or the internet is horrible? Plan B, always
have a plan B."

– "Duly noted." Deep inside, I disagree. I have prepared
spare batteries, chargers, additional phones and 3G cards.
Nothing will go wrong. I manage it. Yet… Charles doesn't
seem to be wrong very often and I can't argue that having a
plan B is a bad thing…

– "What about screw drivers?" I must have raised my
eyebrows a little too much as Charles adds "Come on
Andrew, don't tell me you haven't planned ANY toolbox!"

– "Screw drivers…? What for?"

– "Duh! For repairing! Say your samples break down or
one of your banners isn't properly hanging… having a
couple of screw drivers is essential on a booth, don't go
without! Same with a boxcutter, scissors, tape, and so on."

– "Ok, I will   "

Charles continues:

– "… and it also applies to cleaning products! A broom,
some cleaning cloth, window spray… the basics! You need
to keep your booth fresh throughout the entire event."

– "Got it!"

– "What about business cards?" This time, I know I am up
to his expectations:

– "Ready! 100 cards per person as well as 200 'standard'
cards for those visitors who don't represent serious leads."

– "Perfect! What about drinks?"

– "You mean… at the booth?"

– "Yes of course!"

– "Well… there is a cafeteria at the corner so…"

– "Andrew, do you have any idea how expensive it will be there? Didn't you tell me you are already 15% over budget? Did you account for the on-spot expenses? Food, drinks, cabs... I bet you will end up 30% over your budget!"

– "Damn... I did not think about that..."

– "Look, these events are exhausting. You need your whole team properly hydrated and you don't want them to purchase an expensive coffee every hour. Buy 1.5L of water per person per day and store it on your booth. You will both save money and improve your team's efficiency."

– "Sounds like a smart idea."

Charles goes on and on about the trade show toolbox I need to prepare. There are so many things I did not think about. Suddenly, he changes topic:

– "What about the carpet?!"

– "What about it?"

– "Did you pick a thick or thin carpet?"

I did not expect that question. I'm not even sure to remember what I have picked, that was such a long time ago.

– "Thick... I think..."

– "Oh, Andrew..." Charles put his head in his hands, obviously discouraged. How could the thickness of the carpet be THAT important...? "Andrew, your booth carpet must always be thin. First, because it is much easier to clean, but mostly because you will stand on it for the whole duration of the show."

– "And...? Wouldn't thick carpet be more comfortable...?" I say, quite suspicious.

– "Comfortable in the short run, maybe. But you will be standing on a thick carpet for 3 entire days – trust me, your legs will beg for mercy!" He might be right, I did not think about that. "And have you picked your outfit yet?" Changing topic again… quite difficult to follow his thinking.

– "My outfit…? Yes, I guess. My usual suit and I just bought a new pair of shoes to look perfect on that day."

– "Forget about your new shoes! A trade show is the worst place on earth to try new shoes. Only use shoes you are comfortable with – especially if you are using thick carpets".

Charles keeps talking about my shoes and the carpets while my brain disconnects for a while and I start thinking about all this work I still have to do and the very limited time I have left.

– "Andrew? Andrew? You're still with me?"

– "Yes, sorry, I'm here. I was lost in my thoughts again…"

– "I was asking if you've already prepared your follow-up emails".

– "Yes, I have. Different templates for different types of leads."

– "Perfect! Don't forget to personalize them a little before sending it out!"

– "Sure will."

– "Ok, so now let's discuss your daily routine."

– "My daily routine? You mean, in the booth? Talking to

visitors, right?"

– "You are the project lead, the 'booth manager'. You have more to do than just talk to visitors!" I should have expected this: there is always more to come. What is it this time? "You must be the first to arrive at the booth in the morning. Have you and your team go through a quick clean up, make sure there is no dust on your samples. Then, go through a morning pep talk."

– "A pep talk? I'm not good at that. I will probably be the least experienced one in the booth, shouldn't someone else…?"

– "No, it has to be you. You don't build credibility with your age or outlook. Credibility comes from trust – look confident, know your topic, prepare everything well and people will listen to you. A morning pep talk is essential to motivate your troops and remind them of their daily objectives."

– "I still think that…" he doesn't let me finish.

– "After that, give hourly feedback to your team – number of leads collected, most active staff, goal completion percentage, etc. Keep them involved, motivated, excited! Half of the job is done if you can achieve that. And don't forget to keep your boss in the loop – he will definitely want regular updates."

I am now taking some notes. I should have done this from the first minute: I came for a relaxing coffee and end up taking a master class and I did not even take proper notes! How am I going to remember all this?

– "At the end of each day, do not close your booth before

the official time. Once all the visitors have gone, have your team clean up the stall. Before they leave, have a debrief session: what went right, what went wrong, what should be improved."

– "It means they will need to stay behind and work some extra hours, isn't it?"

– "That's trade shows, it's always like that. Plan some additional budget to invite the team to a nice restaurant, have a drink or something. But do NOT allow them to get drunk or party overnight. You need them fresh and ready by the morning!"

– "Wow, that's a lot to control… organizing an exhibition stall feels more and more like being a general in the army…!"

– "That's the spirit" says Charles with a smile. He waves at the waitress who brings the bill. He pays for the drinks and we're on our ways. Just before saying goodbye, he adds:

– "And don't forget to set your email auto-reply next week." I must look quite worried because he says "Come on Andrew, that's going to be a lot of fun!"

Chapter 13.
FIRST DAY IN THE BOOTH

That's it. 6 months of preparation, stress, excitement and frustrations are now over. Today is the first day of the exhibition. I woke up at 4am and couldn't go back to sleep. I reviewed my plan and all my documents, tried to have breakfast but couldn't eat anything.

I am the first one in the booth this morning – I arrive at 7am when the doors open. When I arrive at the stall all our cartons are there, waiting for me. But nothing is ready. The samples haven't been positioned, tools, cleaning products and bottles of water are still packed and there is dust all over the place. The lights are off, it seems some electrical connections are missing. Panicked, I call Karen:
– "Where are you???"
– "Home… what's going on Andrew, you sound panicked." she says, obviously just waking up.
– "Nothing is ready! There's no light, the cartons are still on the floor, the samples haven't been placed and…"

– "Calm down Andrew… the fair opens at 10. I will be there in an hour and I will call the electrician on the way. Start taking care of the cartons, I'll be there shortly." She hangs up. Am I less worried? A little maybe.

I decide to take the lead and start managing the booth. I reach out for my toolbox – thank you Charles for your bright ideas! I get a cutter and start opening cartons. I place samples on the furniture as per Karen's plan, flatten cartons and store them in the cabin, sweep the floor, dust the place and get things organized.
– "Hello. I'm here for the light, what's the problem?" asks a man, early forties, well-fitting overalls and his very own toolbox in his hand. That must be Karen who arranged it.
– "Well… there's no light in our booth! We've requested having two halogens in the back there as well as spotlights here, there and back there" I point around the booth with my finger.
– "And…?" he asks, disenchanted or simply bored.
– "And it obviously isn't working!"
The man remains calm. He hasn't moved. He's chewing something and takes a few second to respond to me.
– "Have you tried the switch?"
-"The… what? What switch?"
– "As per your floor plan, we've installed a switch in the cabin. Have you tried pressing it…?"
I can feel myself turning pale as blood tries and escape from my face. Did I even check if there was a switch in the booth? No, I have not. Without a word I run through the

stall, open the cabin's door and press the button. Nothing happens. Somehow victorious, I claim:

– "See? Not working!"

– "Am on it." he says casually.

15 minutes later, Karen arrives:

– "Wow! Nice! You've prepared everything already, well done!"

– "Thank you. But the light still isn't working."

– "Don't worry so much Andrew, we'll get there. Have you heard of Murphy's law? It says that…"

– "… everything that can go wrong will go wrong, yeah, I know" I say somehow frustrated.

– "Well great then!" she says with a smile, obviously in a very good mood. "I go get some breakfast, should I get you a coffee?"

I can't believe she is leaving already.

– "Yeah, grab me a cup please. No cream, no sugar."

– "Consider it done"

When the team arrives it is already 9.15. 45 minutes to go before the opening and the booth is ready: light is now working, all the samples are neatly organized and there is no more dust on the floor. It is time for me to start the show.

– "Ok guys, please regroup here". There are 5 people in our team – myself, Karen, a young salesperson from my team who I really seldom talk to and 2 additional part-timers we've recruited and trained already. They all come around me. I'm no public speaker and I usually feel extremely anxious talking in front of people. But today is different. Today, I'm in charge. Today, I can't let anything go wrong and I WANT to lead this project.

– "Thank you for being here. But please, be on time! Tomorrow, the show will start at 9am. I expect all of you to be here at 8.30, no later than that." I try to look serious and credible. I am not really sure whether I am doing a good job there.

– "Today is the first day of the event. I hope you are all full of energy. There are a few important key points I want to remind you of. First, no eating, no drinking and definitely no phone playing, checking or anything. Don't stare at your shoes, look the visitors in the eyes, smile and be welcoming. Don't stand at the edge of the booth like you're guarding the border. Find ways to make people want to come and talk to you." as I talk, I am gaining confidence. I see that everyone is paying attention and that gives me additional courage. Karen is looking at me like a proud mother looking at her kid on his graduation day – it feels kind of weird but I have no time to think about it.

– "I believe you all know your goals already, but let me remind them to you. You are here to qualify and capture leads."

My boss arrives in the booth and I stop talking as I see him coming.

– "Don't stop, don't stop! Please go on."

I continue my speech for another two minutes, thank

everyone for listening and wish everyone good luck. Once I am done, everyone turns to my boss:

– "Don't look at me! Everything you see here has been organized by Andrew. For the coming three days, he is the boss. Any decision or question, go to him." A vote of confidence from my CEO – that was all I needed. He comes to me while others disperse in the booth.

– "Morning pep talk, ah?" he says with a smile. "Great idea. Now don't be shy – do what you think necessary to get things right and I will support you if you need it."

At 10.05am, visitors start flowing through the aisles of the fair. I feel the pressure growing like if I was about to go on stage. One visitor passes by our booth without looking at us, then a second one and a third. The fourth visitor makes eye contact with me and greets me with smile. That's it. That my turn. I try to remember I am a sales person before all and decide to engage the conversation.

– "Good morning sir! Do you already use our products?"

– "Good morning. No, I must say I don't but we have similar ones in our collection." I hooked him! Things start pretty well for me, now I must make sure I don't lose this one – all my team is now looking at me.

– "Oh really? May I ask you which ones you currently have?"

I spend 10 minutes with this visitor. The conversation is nice and interesting. He is already selling similar products from one of our competitors. I show him our features and we discuss pricing. I am not sure whether I could convince him to ride with us instead but there seem to be an opportunity.

After he leaves the booth, I grab my tablet, open my leads collection tool and start recording data. I scan his business card, take some notes, add a few tags to identify and categorize him, send him a quick thank-you email and put the tablet back in the cabin. When I return to the booth, 3 more visitors are looking at our products. One of them is talking with Karen, the other two are left alone. I go to the other sales person:

– "What are you waiting for? There are visitors unattended here." He looks at me, uncomfortable.

– "They did not look at me. I guess that means they don't want to talk yet…"

– "Don't give yourself excuses. Jump on it!"

Unwillingly, he approaches one of the visitors. The promoters we hired saw that and one of them immediately takes action and goes talk to the other visitor. Things start to work as planned!

It is now 11.30am. I log on to our event management tool to see the status – 12 leads captured, 3 of them are serious, 4 are valid, the others would probably lead nowhere. I check everyone's performance and go talk with my team.

– "Hey Karen."

– "Hi Andrew!" she replies with a smile. "Not bad, right? We did quite a good job!"

– "Yes, things are going well so far. Look, I just wanted to let you know you've captured 3 leads already, you have reached 50% of your objective today and you are the most efficient team member so far. Keep going!"

– "What about the global number? Are we on track?"

– "Kind of… We should have 30 by the end of the day, we are only at 12 so far… but we haven't reached half of the day yet, so everything's still possible!"

– "You are right. But make sure you talk to everyone and give some advice to the rest of the team. Especially the two promoters – they don't seem to be too active, they definitely need some pushing from your side."

– "I am going to do that, thank you." After talking with everyone, I decide to talk to my boss:

– "Hey Andrew, how is it going?"

– "Quite well actually… 12 leads so far, we're on the right track to reach our daily objective."

– "Good to hear! Have you counted my leads as well?" Damn, I forgot to teach him how to use our system. He is probably using pen & paper still.

– "I guess I did not… maybe I could show you the system we use? It would be very efficient if you could use the same with us!"

– "Haha, I'm not too keen on learning new things Andrew, I think I'll pass" he says laughing.

– "I understand, but I'm sure you would love it and save some extra time!" He apparently likes me to be persistent:

– "Ok Andrew, you win. Show me that system of yours."

I give him a quick demo on how to scan the business card, add some notes and save it all. I must have convinced him as he says:

– "Wow, that's much easier than expected! Great, I'm definitely going to use it! You know what, I'm even going to input the leads from this morning right now so that we have it all in one place."

– "That would be great, thank you!"

Karen reaches out:

– "You guys want lunch? I am going to grab sandwiches for everyone."

I look at my watch: 12.30 already. I was so busy getting things done I completely forgot about lunch.

– "That would be great, ham and cheese for me please. Make sure you keep the bill though!"

– "Haha, I will Andrew."

– "Same for me" says my boss. "Andrew, you want to give some instructions to the team regarding lunch?"

– "Oh, yes, you're right! Karen, please don't let them eat in the booth – we take lunch break one at a time and eat either in the cabin or elsewhere".

– "You got it!" she says while leaving the stall to go buy some food.

It is now 6pm, people start leaving the show. There are no more visitors in our booth so I decide to gather the team.

– "You guys did great today! We were planning on getting 30 leads and we reached 42."

There is a round of applause.

– "However, there is room for improvement. Some of

these leads are of no value. One of you guys spent almost 30 minutes talking with a retailer from Canada. We're neither selling in Canada nor working directly with retailers. Keep in mind the filtering process we've discussed: find out who they are, what they do and their potential working with us. If the person does not meet our criteria, thank them politely and move on to the next visitor."
– "Also, I would like to highlight some key elements today. I have noticed one of you with a chewing-gum this morning – I can't accept that. As long as you are in this booth, you represent the company. I repeat once again: no playing with your phone, no eating, no drinking, no sitting and definitely no chewing gum in the booth, alright?"
I quickly look at my boss who nods. He really trusts me with that and it makes me feel stronger.
– "In terms of individual results, Jerry, you need to do better – only 4 leads today." Jerry is one of the 2 promoters we've recruited. He looks at his shoes when hearing his name.
– "It's ok, that was the first day. You will do better tomorrow. Be more confident, go talk to people, don't wait for them to come.".
– "I will" Jerry says.
– "And thank you Karen who is the champion of the day! 9 leads collected, well done!"
Karen raises her arms in victory.
– "Ok guys, that was great but we need to do even better tomorrow. Please all grab a cloth or a broom and help cleaning the booth. That will be done in 5 minutes if

everyone helps and we can all go home and relax!"

As I grab some window cleaning spray, my boss comes to me:
– "You see Andrew, 6 months ago, you had no idea what trade shows were all about. Today, you proved I was right to give you this project. Keep doing great work and you can be sure that your future will be bright in this company!"

Chapter 14.
LAST DAY IN THE BOOTH

Finally, the last day has come.

I arrive at the booth at 8am, one hour before opening. I start by cleaning up the stall but there isn't much to do – my team was pretty efficient last night.

I decide to have a look around and talk with other exhibitors before visitors arrive. There is a booth, not far from mine, at the corner of an aisle, that has a really great design. They have built walls for the back of their stall with exhibit windows – one product per display, good lighting, and a small foam board explaining what the product does. It really looks great and drives me to their booth to look closer.

– "Hi there!" a member of their team approaches me. "You are exhibiting also, right? It seems I have seen you guys' booth yesterday."
– "Right. We're on the other side actually. So how has it been for you? Was the exhibition successful?"
– "It was not bad. Quite some traffic, a lot of inquiries and potential business. We're quite satisfied."

– "Well your booth looks really great, no wonder you attracted many people."
– "Thank you. It took a lot of work to make happen but it was worth all our sweat!"
– "So how many leads have you captured?"
He reaches out to the shelf behind him and grabs a large folder with sheets of paper poorly arranged.
– "Here you go!"
– "What is that…?" I ask, dubious.
– "These are our leads!" he claims with a smile. He opens the folder; a few sheets drop on the floor. Pointing at the content, he says:
– "We have been quite efficient, look! There must be at least a hundred fifty leads here!"
The leads papers come in every possible shape and size. Some are even written on napkins from the nearby coffee shop. Some have a business card stapled in a corner, others don't. Some are covered with text, others only have a few words.
– "Wow, that's quite a success" I say politely. He looks very proud and does not seem to notice my doubts. "How long do you think it will take for you to follow-up all that…?"
– "Well, we are pretty organized. We have a team of three interns that will take over next week. It should take them no more than 3 days to put everything into excel and then another couple of days to send emails. All in all, it should be done within 10 days."

10 days. He claims it with pride. Isn't 10 days incredibly long? And looking at the pile of leads, I am wondering if they could really do any follow-up at all – some of them seem frankly unreadable. How could an intern read these notes and guess what to do with it?

– "Interesting" I say.

– "How many did you guys get?"

I reach out for my pocket and grab my phone. He frowns for a second then gets closer to look at my screen. I open my browser and show him our leads statistics:

– "We have captured 103 leads until now and I expect another 45 by the end of the day."

His eyes widen as he looks at my screen:

– "You guys spend so much time making graphs and yet you have time to capture leads? How do you do that? You have interns as well I bet!" he says with a smirk.

– "No interns actually. And we don't make graphs ourselves. We use a system to record the leads digitally and it helps us keeping track of our count easily."

– "Digitally?" he asks, hesitant. "Isn't it taking much longer to record details?"

– "It actually isn't. We scan business cards, click a few buttons and add a few notes, that's about it. It takes a couple minutes each time and saves us three days of data entry afterward."

– "Smart…" he says, lost in his thoughts. "So you actually follow-up within less than 5 days I imagine?"

– "Less than that. We send instant follow-up emails through our system. We have pre-written email templates and we just customize them a little before sending out to make it more personal and add a couple of pictures. We are becoming experts in selfies now!" I say laughing.

He really looks surprised:

– "I have been attending fairs for the past 10 years and have never heard of such system! That's incredible! Did you guys develop it in-house?"

– "No, it is an online service actually. There are quite a few similar solutions out there, you should have a look."

– "Trust me, I will!" he replies, excited.

I keep walking the aisles and take notes of all the smart things I see in other booths. Some of these companies have a giant circular banner hanging from the ceiling. From what they told me, it is quite affordable and might be a great idea for our next event.
One of them has prepared a big wheel for some kind of game and a promoter with a lapel microphone invites attendees to come by giving it a try.
Another one has some kind of photo booth where people can take selfies and post them on Social Media.
There is one that has reproduced a shop shelf and organized products on it like if it was in a supermarket. Quite a smart idea to let buyers feel what it would look like in-store, I guess.

As I see a few visitors walking by I realize the show is already open and run back to my booth.
– "Andrew! Where were you?! I had to do the morning speech myself!" says Karen, looking angry yet relieved to see me.
– "I was walking around. I got a few smart ideas for our next expo!"
– "One thing at a time Andrew – focus on capturing leads today, we'll think about the next expo when the time comes."

It is now 7pm and we are all packing our samples in carton boxes. Luckily, Karen and I thought of everything and the return shipment has already been booked. That was definitely a smart move considering the huge queue in front of FedEx office.

Everyone looks exhausted but happy – it will probably take another 30 minutes to tidy up the place and then it will all be over.

As I put tape on a carton I receive a message from my boss: "Great job Andrew! I've been looking at the stats, it looks like you've captured more leads than we expected! Gather the team and join me downstairs, I'll invite you all out to a restaurant!"

Everyone is here, sitting around the large table, with a glass of wine in the hand.

– "I would like to thank you all for the great work. You have all been performing beyond expectation. And I would like to thank Andrew who did amazing – that was his very first trade show, yet he managed it like a pro! Right, Andrew?"

I really appreciate the compliment but am not too comfortable being pushed into the spotlight by my boss.

– "Yes, I guess." I say, as I turn red.

– "Come on! Don't be shy! I was expecting about a hundred leads, yet you guys captured 196! And all have been followed-up already! That is definitely the best event we've had so far!"

I want to intervene and remind him that we can't consider the leads "followed-up" quite yet. Yes, we sent an email to keep the conversation going but there's still some sales work to do to convert these people into customers. I finally decide it isn't worth it: everyone is happy, let's not spoil the moment.

I look at Karen but she doesn't seem upset our boss did not congratulate her also. Quite the contrary – she looks thrilled that the event was such a success.

– "Alright guys, enjoy your meal, have a few drinks and

relax this weekend – Monday there will be a lot of work waiting for you!"

Chapter 15.
BACK TO THE OFFICE

It is 9am and I am walking into the office.

Some people are already on the phone, others are staring at their screen with a cup of coffee in the hand. Some seats are still empty. I pass by Karen's desk but it is still empty. When was the last time she and I arrived AFTER everyone else in the office?

I arrive at my desk, turn on my screen and go make a coffee while my computer starts.

- "Hi Andrew! How was the weekend?" my boss is already here, which is quite unusual for a Monday morning.
- "It was great, thank you for asking" I say with a smile. "How was yours?"
- "Terrific! I'm glad the event is behind us. You must be relieved too, aren't you?" he says, obviously teasing me.
- "Well... I will be. Soon. But there is still work to do!"
- "Oh, really?" he says, genuinely surprised. "What is there for you to do now?"
- "We have sent automatic emails to all our leads, and it

was a great initiative to make sure they don't forget us, but I'm afraid that won't be sufficient to generate business. Now I want to organize our leads based on qualification criteria we defined earlier with Karen and start following up more thoroughly."

- "I see... and when do you believe you will be able to do that?" he asks, cunning.

- "Well, I will filter our leads today then wait for another day or two to follow-up, see if people answer my first email before spamming them again."

- "We'll see about that!" he says while leaving me, laughing. What does he mean? What is the problem exactly?

As I sit at my desk, I put my hot coffee on the side, open my mailbox, take a sip and... nearly choke. 458 emails. All unread.

I nearly forgot that with the booth planning, the event itself and all the side projects I have neglected my mailbox a little. I decide to go to the essential and go through email subjects to highlight those that require urgent follow-up. All these where I am only in copy end-up in a different box I will check... later.

It already 2pm. I am still going through my emails and I haven't had lunch yet when my stomach starts growling. I decide to go downstairs buy a sandwich when I bump into Karen:

- "Hi there! How are you doing?"
- "Quite busy actually, I thought I would qualify all the

leads today but..."

- "Yeah, about that..." Karen does not let me finish, she looks somehow upset. "Look, my mailbox is full and I can't seem to be able to empty it so it looks like I won't be able to do my part after all."

- "Same here" I say, appeased to not be the only one in this situation. "Here is the plan: just focus on REALLY important emails and clear them up. For all the less important stuff, postpone them a little. I will manage to get you the list by the end of the day - all you have to do is plan the campaign to be sent out tomorrow during lunch time: that's it."

- "I'm not sure if..." Karen tries to turn my offer down but I won't let her.

- "We have spent SO much time and effort working on this project. There is NO WAY a full mailbox stands between us and victory, alright?" I can feel my hands trembling. It seems I am losing control and getting angry against my will. It may be a good thing as Karen suddenly seems to agree with me:

- "You're right! Let's get done with it! I will clear my mailbox while you prepare the list for me. Hey, where are you going by the way?"

- "Heading out to buy a sandwich. You want me to get you something?"

- "Make it two!"

As part of our trade show strategy, Karen and I hashed out a plan where we would qualify the leads and break them into three categories:

- hot leads - to be urgently followed-up by me
- warm leads - second priority, but still managed by me individually
- cold leads - these are not ready to buy and Karen will manage them with a simple EDM

As I take a bite of my sandwich, I open our leads file and start looking through the 196 contacts we collected. Luckily, we had the smart idea to using tags and filtering leads is just about clicking a few buttons: order by lead quality (hot, warm, cold), order by type of prospect, order by size of the potential contract... done!

Originally, Karen planned a one-size-fits-all EDM. It was already setup and ready to send out before the show. Unfortunately, we did not consider the fact that there would be many types of cold leads and this "one-fits-all" strategy does not make much sense anymore.

Karen is creating a few different EDMs with various messages and calls to action based on the type of leads we captured.

My lists are finished, I head towards Karen's desk to share it with her.
- "Why do I have to wait?! Did you not see this email was important?!"
My boss is yelling. Apparently, he has a problem with

Karen and I feel like it is somehow related to me. She does not move, staring at her feet, apparently about to cry.
- "Sir?" I dare to interrupt. A few weeks ago, I would have been looking at my feet, hoping his anger wouldn't suddenly come my way. But today I am a different person. I know what it takes to manage complex projects, to handle people's expectations and deal with 10 problems at once. Today, I am no longer shy and obedient: I have an opinion and I want people to know it!

He turns his head in my direction, looking threateningly at me.
- "I am sorry but I really need Karen's help to finalize the leads follow-up communications." He is obviously not used to having people responding to him and let me continue. "We have all spent so much time and efforts on this project. The company has invested so much money." I can feel I have stricken the right cord as he seems to ease off a little. "It would be a shame to throw all that in the trash now that we are so close to our goal. Please give us half a day to finalize everything and we will both go back to our routine tasks."

He does not answer immediately. He seems to be considering my request but very concerned about not losing face. After a few seconds of silence, he turns back to Karen with a soft voice and says:
- "I want a reply no later than 11 am tomorrow." then turns back and walk towards his desk. What a great victory!
- "Wow, you saved me here" says Karen, still shaking.

- "Don't mention it. I got us another half day but realistically it will take me 5 to follow-up with everyone. I can't even imagine what those people taking pen and paper notes are going through!"

- "Let's keep our focus on the task at the moment. You got the list?"

- "Yes, I have it." I pass her a USB stick with all the leads she must follow-up. "This is your part. Manage it quickly so you could go back to your normal job. I will handle the rest."

- "Thank you, Andrew". She looks at me and, as I am not leaving, asks: "Is there something else?"

- "There is. Listen, I know you are very busy and all but... I need a favor."

- "What is it?"

- "Can you please go one last time through the budget and expenses sheet? I want to make 100% sure nothing is missing while it is still fresh in your mind. Later you won't remember everything."

- "Will do." She turns back and sits at her desk, ignoring my presence.

It took me three complete afternoons following-up the 34 hot leads and 52 warm leads we collected. I emailed all of them, call many and set up some meetings. I had to stay behind every day of the week to catch-up with my normal emails.

It is already 11pm when I arrive home and I realize I haven't called Charles a single time since the event. If someone deserves feedback, it is him!

- "Hi Charles, it's Andrew. Am I interrupting something?"
- "Hi Andrew! No, you're not! Glad to hear your voice, how are things going on your side?"
- "I'm sorry I did not call earlier, it's just that..."
Charles laughs very loudly over the phone.
- "Don't worry! I'm sure you are drowning right now! Between your daily tasks, all the work that accumulated while you were at the show and your follow-up job, you must be very busy!" He suddenly becomes much more serious: "You ARE following-up as I taught you, right?"
- "Yes, yes, I am. I was, actually. I'm done now."
- "Congratulations! Your job is done! All you have to do is keep pushing these leads like you would any other sales lead."

Charles and I keep talking for another hour, sharing anecdotes and stories from the exhibition then I head to bed, happy that the event is now behind us.

Chapter 16.
6 MONTHS POST-EVENT

- "Everyone, please, sit down." my boss presides over the meeting. He has invited every department's Head. We all have an assigned seat and I am just in front of him, on the other side of the table, Karen by my side.

I haven't really had a chance to work with her lately. Six months have passed since our last meeting to follow-up with the trade show leads and things have gone back to normal. She smiled at me when we entered the room but there has been no eye-contact since.

- "The reason why you are all here today is to review the roadmap for the coming 6 months to one year."
Only department heads are usually part of this meeting. They discuss strategy, objectives, recruitment.

People of my grade have never been invited to join. It must be a first for Karen as well since she seems disoriented. She tries very hard to look like she belongs and frowns at every word our boss says.

- "There is no need to keep all of you here the entire morning, which is why I want to start with the major milestone for this semester and release some of you. Andrew, Karen, do you know why you're here?"

Karen jumped when she heard her name, more focused on looking attentive than on really listening.

- "I assume we will join a new trade show and you would like us to lead the project?" I try.
- "Not 'a new' trade show. I want to join HKTDC Hong Kong Electronics Fair again this year. Does everyone agree?" All department heads vigorously shake their head in approval. Not one of them had been involved in the previous event, they probably don't even know what it was all about, but all give an energetic approval.
- "Good, then let's move on to.."
- "I don't agree" I say, cutting my boss in the middle of his sentence.
- "Excuse me?" he says, obviously not happy I would defy him in front of everyone. "You refuse to lead that project?" he asks between his teeth. Other people around the table avoid any direct eye contact with either of us, staring at their hands or pretending to read their notes. Only Karen looks at me, pale, grasping her armrest as if she was about to experience a car crash.
- "Not at all! I would gladly lead such project again!" I say with enthusiasm. "I just think HKTDC Hong Kong Electronics Fair is not the right show for us."
- "What are you talking about?" replies my boss, short-tempered. "It was a great event, we got more leads than ever before, talked to many people and received a lot of positive feedback!"
- "All this is true."

- "Then, end of story!"
- "But..." I continue, ignoring his response. "... data tells us a different story."
I quickly look around the table. Most people are still pretending not to hear anything. Some look fairly annoyed while the one at the right of my boss looks curious and expects me to continue. Karen does not dare move a finger and patiently waits for the torture to end. She must be praying that no-one notices she's here.

- "Do you mind?" I say, pointing at the computer screen in our meeting room.
- "Please go, Andrew, share what you have since it seems we won't be able to avoid it anyway." My boss now seems resigned and annoyed but no longer angry.

I open our trade show dashboard. I had reviewed this scene in my head a hundred times. I knew, sooner or later, I would have the opportunity to show what I had prepared. Today was my turn to shine and I wasn't about to screw it up.

My screen is now shared through the large wall-projector and everyone is looking at it. Using a laser pointer, I show a first graph.

- "You see? Those are the leads we collected at the last edition of that event."
- "Yes, right, we all remember that Andrew! 196 leads, the best score to date, we all know that! So what's your point?" he is obviously very irritated but still wants to know where I am heading.
- "True. We did capture a lot of leads. Now, this figure on

the right is the total amount that we spent for this event."
Overall, Karen managed to keep the event expenditures
within the original budget but it does not seem to make her
feel any better. "If I divide this number by the total number
of leads, I get this new figure: our 'cost per lead'".
- "And...?" my boss asks impatiently.
- "And, on its own, this number does not mean much." I
see him roll his eyes and get ready to jump at my throat.
"But, I took the liberty to compare it with other numbers
that I received from Karen's department" I - and everyone
else - can hear her squeak. No-one pays too much attention,
but I know she now regrets to have shared her data with
me.
- "This is the price we pay for ONE lead through Google
Adwords, and that is what we pay for a lead through cold
calling."
- "These two numbers are slightly lower, that's true, but the
difference isn't significant" says my boss. "What's your
point?"
- "It is true, the difference is rather small. Moreover, those
leads we get through Adwords or cold-calling are fairly high
in our sales funnel while these we got at trade shows are
quite down the funnel already."
- "Precisely, so what is your point?" He definitely lost the
little patience he had left and his face is turning red.
- "I understand you would like me to just spit the answer
but it is important I take you through the whole process for
it to make sense. If you allow me, I will continue."

He sits back in his chair and unwillingly invites me to go on
with a gesture of his hand.

- "See, from a cost-per-lead perspective, the show is more
or less the same as other campaigns we have. Bear in mind

however that Google Adwords are mostly automated and require MUCH less work than a trade show."
- "True..."

Happy to hear him approve, I keep going.

- "Now, what REALLY concerns me is our sales funnel. You see?" I display on the wall a funnel divided into 6 steps: uncontacted, first email, proposal, negotiation, lost and won. "For those of you who may not be familiar with Sales strategies," my boss seem to suddenly realize and regret there are other people in the room, "this is a sales funnel. When we meet a prospect, we put him at the tip of this basket. As the conversation goes, we move him further down towards the 'win' - or 'lose', depending on the situation."

Some of my co-workers seem to be getting a serious headache.

- "Now, the purpose of all this trade show was to capture leads, get them through this funnel and push them further down until converting them into customers."
- "Everyone gets that, Andrew!"

I ignore his comment and keep going.

- "As mentioned earlier, we have captured 196 leads at this event. Out of these, only 2% has been converted." I see him open his mouth and decide to keep going before giving him a chance to interrupt again. "The turnover represented by these 2 % is here, on the right of this chart. The problem is, when taking into account expenses on the left and revenue on the right, we get a Return On Investment

of 100%."
- "That's amazing!" shouts the Head of Design before getting the killer eye from my boss.
- "Not really" I reply. "100% ROI means we JUST covered our expenses, we did not make any profit. And this does not even count all the work the organization represented or the actual profit: we are talking of gross revenue only!"
- "You are telling us you haven't done your job as sales and it resulted in a fiasco?!" yells my boss, searching for someone to blame. I keep my calm: I had expected and rehearsed this situation, I know exactly how to react.
- "No. As you can see from this funnel, most leads have been followed-through multiple times, as expected. None of them remains on the top of the funnel and we have used the same techniques that usually work. The problem does not come from our sales strategy."
- "What then?!"

Everything went exactly as I planned it. Even though my stomach is upside down, nothing can be detected on my face. I look calm and confident and will go through the situation: there is no way back anyway!

- "Please have a look at this graph" He yells "what now?!" as I point at the wall.
- "These are the 'tags' we used during the event. We used these labels to easily qualify and identify prospects. You can see things such as 'hot lead', 'cold lead', 'distributor', 'retailer', etc. Each prospect has a few labels that help us identify him."
- "For god sake, Andrew, DO YOU HAVE A POINT?!!"
- "We went to this event looking for distributors. Look at the graph. Less than 10% of our booth visitors were actually distributors. 35% were wholesalers, 22% were

distributors and the rest were agents, competitors, random visitors..."

My boss keeps his mouth wide open. He obviously needs some time to digest the information.

- "I had the feeling most people I talk to were actually distributors... Are you SURE about what you are saying?" he says slowly, staring at my graphs.

- "Absolutely sure. You had the 'feeling' that most people were retailers because we had much longer chats with this 10% of our visitors than with the other 90%."

- "So... this year, the audience of the show was not the right one. That is what you are saying?"

- "I actually believe the same thing has been happening for the past few years as well. The only difference is that this year we DO have statistics and data. As you said, the event went well, we received great feedback, we all had 'the feeling' that there were plenty of distributors at the show... all this is only appearance, feelings, ideas. When we start looking into real data, things look very different."

My boss looks completely devastated.

- "Andrew, if what you say is true, we have been wasting tons of money for the past 10 years! Are you saying we should never participate in trade shows again?"

- "That is not what I am saying. Trade shows are great! These are probably the best place for us to get new business. However, if we join only one show per year, we should select it based on the audience we expect to reach. In our case, I made some research and there is another event, very similar, in Germany that may be a better fit..."

- "Hi Andrew, how are you?"
- "Hey Charles, I'm glad you call! How are things going for you?"
- "Doing good, doing good... I wanted to congratulate you for your promotion but... I can't hear you too well, where are you right now?"
- "Sorry Charles, I'm at CeBIT right now, in Germany. Just finished training with the temp staff I recruited, make sure they know how to use our lead capture tool efficiently!"
- "Wow, that is amazing! Maybe we could grab a drink when you come back so you could tell me your story! Will you be back next week?"
- "Sorry, it will have to wait another month. I am travelling to Las Vegas next, for another electronic show. I convinced my boss to join 2 this time, I had great data to backup my claim!"
- "Well, I wish you the best Andrew, seems you came a long way since your call a year ago. Let me know when you're in town, we have lots of things to discuss!"
- "Sure, talk to you soon".

As I hang up the phone, I see Karen running towards me: some new problems to deal with.

TAKEAWAY

I did not want to end the Trade Show Chronicles without giving you some actionable takeaway.
Every business is different and everyone's story is unique. What Andrew went through may not apply to your own situation and his approach might not be the right one for your company. It really is for you to figure out what makes most sense to achieve your goals and reach your targets.

Yet, the backbone of every good trade show strategy is always the same and the different pieces that compose this strategy remain very similar.
In this section I will review some key elements from Andrew's story that you could apply directly to your next trade show. The goal is to give you short and practical tips that could forever change your trade show management. Up to you to cherry-pick what is relevant to your unique situation.

Always plan in advance - 6 months is not too much to prepare your team for a trade show. But do not waste this precious time with procrastination: the temptation of saying "I have plenty of time, I can worry about this later" can be strong! Start with a checklist of all the things you will need to organize, and setup a calendar to spread these tasks over the given timeline.

Budget everything - a good budget is a clear and early budget. Before arranging anything else, figure out how much money you allocate to this event and break it down into categories (booth rental, marketing, on-site expenses, logistics, etc.) to see whether you can afford attending the show. The best method to do this is to use past budgets from your previous shows and start with the objectives: how much money do you expect to generate from this show?

Record expenses - to avoid overspending you must know control your expenses. Don't wait until the last minute to collect all receipts and figure out how much you spent. Expenses recording must be an ongoing process and should be included in your budget sheet to easily identify whether you are overspending.

Inform your network - people attract people. There is a reason why people avoid empty shops or restaurants: we tend to be attracted by places already populated with people. Reach out to your existing networks of customers, prospects, partners, suppliers and invite them to come pay you a visit. All your booth needs is a sparkle to ignite a big fire.

Update your signature - you and your team send tens if not hundreds of emails each day. Having a banner in your signature costs literally nothing and put your show participation in front of many people's eyes. Try to redirect people clicking on your banner to a page explaining what you will be presenting at the show.

Be smart about your message - informing people that you will exhibit at a show is great. But telling people "come visit us booth ABC" does not have much of an impact. Highlight the reasons why people should visit your booth and focus on communicating those. Are you showcasing new products, innovations? Offering discounts, exclusive offers? Are you planning some games or contest?

<u>Build a booth promotion page</u> - if people are indeed interested in visiting your booth and wish to find out more, don't send them to your website. Chances are that your website will not answer any of their questions. Build a standalone "booth presentation page" instead. A targeted page that explains who you are, why you participate in the event, how to find you, what you will present, why people should come visit, etc. is what you need. Give people the ability to request an appointment with you.

<u>Set targets</u> - defining objectives serves three purposes: motivating your team (people tend to be more productive when they have a quantifiable goal), giving a clear direction for everything that follows and enabling you to estimate your success. Your targets should be set long before the show so that you all have a goal to work toward.

<u>Select the right booth</u> - choosing a booth is never an exact science, but some elements never change. Try to be in the most relevant section, always prefer a large alley, pick a booth with multiple openings and find yourself close to major perks and attractions. Some people consider it is better to be on the right side of the entrance based on human behavioral patterns.

<u>Pick your carpet</u> - thick carpets will be comfortable for your visitors but a nightmare for your staff. Prefer thin carpets with good under padding. In terms of color, find something that relates to your brand and clearly contrasts with the aisle's carpet. A well picked carpet will save your energy and help you stand out, so take the time to select the right one.

<u>Leave some empty space</u> - you want your booth to look nice and appealing, but sometimes less is more. Don't over-estimate your stall's size: keep things neat and avoid unnecessary clutter that could limit the flow of visitors.

<u>Put your products in the light</u> - the venue's ambient light is never enough to showcase your product. Consider adding additional spot lights focused on your key products. Prefer LED to halogens to have a cleaner light and avoid over heating your booth.

<u>Plan for internet</u> - very few venues offer decent Wi-Fi at trade shows, and almost none offers FREE decent Wi-Fi. Plan for it yourself, either by ordering a private network from the organizer or by arranging 3G/4G cards. Internet is important to remain connected, check your emails, show your website, relevant videos, capture leads, share on Social Media, etc.

<u>Have a floorplan</u> - you will have a much better vision of your booth with a floorplan. Add a small character in your booth to see whether you can easily circulate around the products. This floorplan will be shared with all your suppliers to identify the location of furniture, electrical sockets, spotlights, etc. Don't neglect this aspect of your organization.

<u>Prepare your toolbox</u> - as Charles said, Murphy's law is always right. Prepare pens, paper, stapler, glue, tape, scissors, screw driver, batteries, cables, etc. Anything that MacGyver could consider vital should be in your toolbox. On a higher level, have a plan B and some buffer in your budget in case things would go wrong.

<u>Plan your logistics needs</u> - if you send your products or samples by sea instead of air, it will take much longer to arrive, but you may save up to 90% of the cost. All you need to make it happen is to plan early. Don't forget to plan for the return trip: if you do not book your goods post-show logistics you will need to battle with other exhibitors, lining up in front of the local FedEx, UPS or DHL office and pay unexpectedly high expenses.

<u>Figure out your follow-up strategy</u> - following-up with your prospects is the very key to success but needs to be planned ahead of time. Have a set of follow-up emails ready for all possible buyer persona or situation. When it is time for you to actually send follow-up emails, you should only have to select a template and customize it a little. If you must build it from scratch, prepare PowerPoints, and figure out which file to send, you have failed to plan your follow-up properly and you will lose your edge over other exhibitors.

<u>Prepare marketing collaterals</u> - you will most certainly need brochures, catalogs, leaflets, pricelists, product descriptions, etc. Preparing these documents takes time, therefore you must start early. Also consider printing time and logistics. Most of all make sure you have a digital version ready on the cloud and setup some QR codes to easily share them around. If you run out of printed material or if your visitors no longer want to carry documents, having a digital version ready will come handy!

<u>Do you need promoters?</u> - not every booth needs promoters or hostesses. If you have sufficient staff in your team, better use them than hire outsiders. If you do hire promoters, think about what they should wear (the concept

of "booth-babes" may be considered normal for an automotive show but inappropriate for other exhibitions), what training they need, what are your actual expectations, etc. Promoters can have a heavy impact on your budget; therefore you must carefully consider this investment and the expected outcome.

Think about training - even Olympic athletes require training, so there is no reason you and your team should be exempted. Figure out what kind of training you need and how to make sure everyone benefits from it. At the very least, everyone present in your booth should have an intense training covering how to behave in the stall, how to greet people, how to qualify prospects, how to capture leads, how to make a demo, as well as extensive training on the products and benefits.

Teach booth etiquette - there are some basics you need your team to understand and respect. Things you cannot do in a booth, such as chewing gums, eating, drinking, sitting, staring at your shoes, playing with your phone, guarding the entrance, looking angry or bored, etc. Educate your team about the right way to behave in a booth: stand up, smile, look people in the eye, greet people who make eye contact, etc.

Make yourself comfortable - you need to look good, yes, but trade shows are not the right place to try on new shoes or uncomfortable pants. Make yourself comfortable because you will need to stand and talk for hours and your personal comfort directly affects your mood.

<u>Keep your booth clean</u> - with all the construction going on around the venue, there will be dust. Clean up your booth at the beginning and at the end of each day to keep it tidy and attractive. You should definitely bring a broom and some basic cleaning items with you.

<u>Have a qualification process ready</u> - it may be true that "all men are created equal", but it certainly doesn't apply to leads and visitors. It is essential that you differentiate a good lead from a bad one within minutes if you don't want to waste your precious time with people that present low to no potential of becoming customers. To achieve that, you need to spend more time listening than speaking - ask the right questions to identify the quality of each visitor. Before the show, prepare a series of questions that your entire team should be using to figure out whether the prospect is serious, has buying and decision power, has a real need for your product, has sufficient knowledge about the market / industry, etc. You need to clearly define what is a hot lead, a warm lead and a cold lead across your team otherwise you and your teammates will use the same words to talk about different things and your follow-up will be extensively slower.

<u>Capture leads the right way</u> - when you capture leads in your booth, remember why you do it. If your goal is to convert prospects, you will need detailed notes. Standardize your capture so that all leads report use the same format and vocabulary to be easily identified, filtered and organized. Collecting business cards cannot be considered capturing leads: you need to take thorough notes about your prospect and his needs. Avoid pen&paper as it requires double work (you will need to transfer everything to digital sooner or later), causes human errors and

seriously delays your follow up. Capture the lead immediately after the visitor has left your booth, even if it means asking the next visitor to wait for a couple of minutes: your memory isn't as sharp as you think.

Follow-up quickly - if you are not able to follow-up immediately because you must prepare an offer or assemble a presentation, at the very least send a thank you email to your prospect within 48h to let him know that you care, that you are reliable, and make sure he does not forget about you. Remember: buyers talk to tens of people, visit hundreds of booths and see thousands of products. Chances that they will remember you are getting thinner each day.

Use rich emails - a good follow-up email has a clearly defined structure. It is short and contains all your prospect needs: a short intro (who you are), a reminder (use details from the conversation to remind him of you), a brief recap of the discussion and a clear CTA (Call To Action) to bring him one step further down your sales funnel. To make the email even more efficient, you can add links and documents (keep only what is necessary, sending 10 files is the best way to get your email in the trash box) as well as photos (pictures of your booth can help him remember your company, a personal profile photo helps with memories of the conversation, pictures of the products help remind him of your offer, and a nice selfie with him re-builds the connection you had earlier).

Setup reminders - if you are not a sales person using a CRM, setup your own follow-up reminders. After sending an email to someone, set a reminder to make sure you send another email or make phone call after a certain period of time. Only that way can you make sure your leads don't fall through the cracks.

Track email opening -before sending another email or calling a prospect, find out whether he has read your previous email. Use email trackers to know whether people read your emails, it makes your follow-up more efficient.

Don't give up - converting a prospect doesn't happen in one shot. In average, it takes three follow-ups to convert a hot lead captured at a trade show. It would take even longer if the lead wasn't mature yet. Don't give up and keep pushing until you get the sales or a clear signal that the buyer isn't interested. For non-qualified leads or called leads, consider passing them to your marketing team to enter a nurturing program.

Track your achievements - what is success if you can't quantify it? Trade shows are great ego and motivation boosts. Everyone is positive, open, talkative and makes big promises; but don't get fooled. Don't trust everything you hear - words don't mean anything, only actions matter. Track your company's achievements (leads captured, converted, revenue generated, media talking about you, etc.) as well as individual results (for each team member) and compare them to your original targets to identify your level of success. Tracking achievement isn't necessarily relevant right after the event and could be done 6 months post-show, once you have a better vision of customer conversion.

Motivate your team - pep talks are important. It is not just about motivating people but also about showing them that you are with them and reminding everyone of their objectives. You have spent a lot of time and money preparing for the show, make sure your people know it and respect it.

<u>Give immediate feedback</u> - don't wait to be back to the office to point out good and bad things. If you catch your colleagues playing with their phone, draw a red line right away. On the opposite, it someone is doing great, don't be short of good words and recognition. The only rule is to be always positive: you don't want to ruin your people's energy or motivation, every comment, even the negative ones, must be brought in a positive manner.

<u>Explore other booths</u> - there is always idle time at trade shows. Walk the aisles to see what others do better than you, in terms of products but also strategy, booth design, product demo, greeting, etc. There is always something to learn or to improve at an exhibition. Make sure you take notes for later.

<u>Make a post-event report</u> - the event is over, you are tired, you have done your part and all you want is close this chapter and move on. But there is one last thing you need to do, and it is essential. You need to put together a post-event report. This isn't some kind of boring report no-one will ever read - this report contains a list of all the things you did wrong, why it went wrong and how to avoid doing it again next time. It also contains everything you did right and how to do it again for the next show. It contains a list of the suppliers you have used as well as your level of satisfaction. It contains a copy of your budget and expenses, your floorplan and product placement, your electrical and lighting blueprint, etc. It contains ideas taken from other booth. It basically contains everything you need

to start planning your next event. Spending a couple of hours more today could save you days of headaches later.

I could have made this list much longer and it could go on and on for pages. I restricted myself to what I consider being the most important or most easily forgotten aspects of a good trade show strategy.

Do you feel ready for your next show?
Pass this book around to people within your team that will attend the show with you - the more prepared they are, the better your results!

ENDORSEMENTS

Matthew Hill
President, Expert, Trainer| The Hill Group

Want to learn how to exhibit successfully? You could find a bunch of checklists, get some tips from your social network, or learn-by-doing (which could take a while).

But if you want a different way to learn best practices for an exhibitor; planning, managing (tasks and people) and executing with efficiency, take a journey through a clever narrative that is packed with real-life situations, issues, and personalities. I am talking about Julien RIO's new book, *The Trade Show Chronicles*.

You won't get Top 10 Lists, or Dos and Don'ts. What you will get is a well developed storyline that follows Andrew, a fictionalized character that any event or trade show manager can relate to. As you travel with Andrew through the complete process of producing a successful exhibit, you will get entertained and educated at the hand of the author, Julien RIO. He knows a lot and knows how to present it in an engaging story format. Enjoy and learn.

Trevor Lewis
Experiential Marketing Strategist | Skyline

The Trade Show Chronicles perfectly depicts the complexities of the trade show industry and how difficult it can be to navigate. Many companies find themselves in situations similar to Andrew's where they are in charge of a large trade show project and have no idea where to start. Whether you are just beginning to manage your company's trade show program or have been in the industry for years – *The Trade Show Chronicles* is a relatable guide that provides crucial information that will help even the most seasoned planner cultivate an impactful trade show program.

Rauno Ramo
Trade Show Business Consultant| Event & Exhibition Subcontractors World Wide

This is a complete masterpiece from A-Z for everyone who plans to exhibit or even visit an event, and make useful notes for future business plans. It is an amazing imaginary journey, and at the same time there´s so much in common with real life companies expo preparations.

Julien Rio is a true event & expo professional and his clear thinking connected to wide personal industry knowledge can be shaped to the form of this great reading experience. You want to be an event pro? Then do not miss this book!

Richard Erschik
Trade Show Expert | TradeshowLeadsToSales.com

Not everyone gets to experience the entire tradeshow, from beginning to end and after. This walk through the complete process will be reminiscent for many readers.

GET THE TRADE SHOW CHRONICLES TO YOUR TEAM

Knowledge is always better when shared! Order copies of The Trade Show Chronicles for your team now to open their eyes to a new world of event management.
If you found this book helpful, get others to benefit from it. It will set the ground rules and make sure you all use the same vocabulary to talk about the same things.

http://www.julienrio.com/TSC